FROM FULFILLMENT
TO PEACE

La Jolla, CA

(858) 452-6849

www.AzimKhamisa.com

WHAT THEY ARE SAYING

"In my counseling and teaching work, clients and students frequently express that self-blame is one of the most difficult things for them to get past. In "From Fulfillment to Peace," Azim Khamisa has written a powerful and spot-on guide to the journey that takes us through the difficult times of our lives, into our souls and then back out into the world. His chapter on Self-Forgiveness is deep, revealing, enlightening and ultimately healing. I will be recommending this book!"

~ Dr. Kathy Hearn - Speaker, Consultant, Facilitator

"There are few individuals who, because of their integrity born from personal experience, have the trustworthy and insightful voice of a guide through life. Azim is such a person. For our ultimate benefit, Azim unselfishly shares the treasured discoveries he has experienced along his journey of life from murder to forgiveness, from forgiveness to fulfillment and today from fulfillment to peace. If bringing greater peace to every element of the world is part of your life's purpose, Azim's new book is a must read. As pivotal as it may be to my legacy as a leader, this is a book that I will leave my children for their fulfillment in their future."

~ Paul M. Nakai, Senn Delaney

"What started as a journey of tragedy has turned into a promise of peace. Those who pick up this book will find their own peace as they are influenced, inspired, and uplifted by one man's journey from devastation to peace. Azim Khamisa guides us as we witness his torment and his courage to heal, to forgive the unforgiveable, and to move to a sacred peace through goodwill friendship, trust, empathy, and compassion. Every year, Azim Khamisa offers his inspirational message of nonviolence to university students in my communication classes, soon to be transitioning to the workforce. Students are moved, inspired, and encouraged by Azim to ask the tough questions that can transform their lives in ways that shift them away from negative emotions such as anger, jealousy, and resentment to emotions such as trust, empathy, and forgiveness. This book is a must read for people seeking practical strategies and soulful wisdom to move through their own resentments or torments to live a life of understanding, forgiveness, and peace."

~ Patricia Geist-Martin, Ph.D.
School of Communication, San Diego State University

"Azim Khamisa is a modern day Gandhi keeping the unity of means and ends in agreement so that he embodies the ultimate beloved global community as he confronts the sources of violence. His new book will heal many ill situations."

~ Lawrence Edward Carter Sr.
Dean of the Martin Luther King Jr. International Chapel
Professor of Religion at Morehouse College

FROM FULFILLMENT TO PEACE

A ROADMAP TO THE SOUL

By Azim N. Khamisa

La Jolla, California

To my son, Tariq, for connecting me with my heart and soul.

To my daughter, Tasreen, and grandchildren, Shahin & Khalil & Miya, for keeping that connection alive.

And to the countless kids who have been touched and who continue to be touched by Tariq's spirit.

ॐ ॐ ॐ

This book could not have seen completion without the help of the following people to whom I offer my most heartfelt thanks.

To Tariq's mother, Almas, for her friendship and support, and for giving birth to two amazing souls, Tasreen and Tariq.

To my son-in-love (as he likes to be called), Mehrdad, for being a great husband and an awesome father.

To my family, for their love and support:

- Dad (posthumous), Mum
- My sister, Neyleen
- My brother, Nazir, his wife Shelina, and their daughter Soraiya
- My deceased sister, Yasmin (may her soul rest in eternal peace), her husband Tony, and their sons Karim, Nazim, and Salim

To Ples Felix, for being my brother and friend, first in grief and now in love, and for his unwavering commitment and partnership in stopping violence among our children and youth.

To Tony Hicks, without whom this story would be incomplete, and for his significant contribution to TKF, as well as the heartfelt foreword of this book.

To Dan Pearson, for his love, friendship, and guidance, and for always being there for me.

To Kit Goldman, for her friendship and contribution to the work and mission of TKF.

To TKF's Board of Trustees present and past (TKF.org). To the TKF staff present and past.

To TKF and its many volunteers, who in so many ways offer support to carry forward the important mission of our work.

To Brian Klemmer (posthumous), Founder of Klemmer & Associates, Inc., for his friendship, support, and "adoption" of TKF, inspiring so many wonderful people to become Seeds of Hope Society members. To Kimberly Zink and the Klemmer staff that offered dedicated support of TKF's work.

To all those who have supported the foundation's work by generously donating their time, treasure and other resources.

To my good friends Mark Fackler and Rich Meyer for their generosity and wisdom.

To the ANK team: Jennifer Ellis, Jim Ellis and Susan Greene.

To Andrea Cagan, for her immensely valuable and skillful editorial review of the manuscript.

To Dianne McKay for her proofreading impeccability.

To Ian McKay for the book's chapter illustrations which depicted wonderfully and artistically the themes of the book.

For Damon Kinnaman for his guidance and expertise on the cover art.

And, finally, a special and well-deserved, profound acknowledgement to my research and writing team Donna Pinto and Jim Ellis. For Donna's passionate pursuit and brilliant research and writing of my book – this could not have been achieved without her. To Jim for his generous and meticulous work – proofreading the manuscript, as well as full production of layout and design. Thank you, Donna and Jim from the bottom of my heart.

To anyone I may have forgotten to acknowledge, I offer you my deepest apology and expression of love.

TABLE OF CONTENTS

FOREWORD

I was honored when Azim wrote me and asked if I would write the foreword to his latest book. Although I've gotten to know Azim, somewhat, over the past 18 years, I was surprised to be tapped for something like this. My surprise was mingled with concern: could I do justice to this task? I'm not a writer, and the ability to express my thoughts, desires or beliefs has been a lifelong struggle for me. I also haven't been out in the world communicating with people and sharing the message of nonviolence, forgiveness and reconciliation, being a "peace warrior," as I know Azim to be.

The majority of my life has been spent inside of California's maximum security prisons struggling to navigate the hyper-sensitive, distortedly negative and altogether alien world of prison life while trying to refrain from succumbing to the institutionalized mind-state of a prisoner. Add to this, I still see myself very much as a work in progress. Granted I'm far from the 14-year-old mental and emotional mess that took the life of Tariq Khamisa all those years ago. But there still is the self-improvement work needed to address the issues that existed before Tariq's life was taken ... issues that are enormous and to be done in an environment where there is no sincere expectation of self-improvement. This all made it harder to identify, let alone address, the myriad of problems that haunted me.

And although I've waded through my childhood issues (and those incurred later on), slowly unpacking the baggage that weighted heavily on my young soul, I can look back with some personal degree of pride at my ability, with some stumbles along the way, mind you, to chip away the calcifying parts of me that would ultimately stunt my personal growth. I still hold some concerns as to whether or not I can bear honestly my thoughts and opinions about those whom I cherish, the worst thing I've ever done and the pain I've caused so many.

I met Azim a year or so after being transferred from California's Youth Security to a prison within California's Department of Corrections. My grandfather had been telling me in letters and on our visits that Azim had expressed that he would like to come see me if I was open to it. I told my grandfather that I would think about it, with no real intention to do that, hoping that the idea of me ever having to meet Azim, the man whose son I had killed, would fade away. Having been tried as an adult at the age of 14 and sentenced to 25 years to life for my crime, I just wanted to be allowed to lose myself in stagnation of what my life had become, and prepare for my future as a young person possibly destined to spend the rest of his life in prison. I didn't want to deal with the added complication of meeting face-to-face with the man whose son I had taken from him. I didn't see what good would come from such a meeting; Tariq would still be gone and, of course, I would still be serving a life sentence.

The truth is I was afraid of to face Azim. Even though I would be 19, even though I had been tried four years previously as an adult, I was still possessed by the fears and immaturity of the child that I was. Taking responsibility for my actions in a courtroom no more made me a man than committing the acts themselves, and I felt unable to make that leap from perceived adulthood to actual adulthood by sitting and visiting with Azim, a man who must hate me in a way that only a parent who had a child taken from them, could.

I was beyond reluctant to let Azim come visit me at that time and content with my non-committal "I'll think about it" to be my only words on the subject. But of course it wasn't. Admirably, Azim continued to float the idea of his one day visiting with me, and my grandfather, to his credit, continued to remind me of Azim's request.

I was never made to feel pressured by the request but encouraged. One day while sitting in my cell during an institutional lockdown that had lasted for several months, I had considered my responsibility to seeing my actions through to their conclusion. I also owed Azim that much I felt: an opportunity for closure that the court process may not have provided.

I didn't know what to expect from a meeting with Azim, but after having him send in a visiting form and go through the institution's process for visiting approval, he, my grandfather and I were finally able to sit down together in the New Folsom state prison visiting room. I was glad that my grandfather had come on that first visit. He and Azim had forged a friendship out of the tragedy of Tariq's murder, as well as my incarceration, and I felt lacking any previous connection to Azim. Because of this I would need to lean on their relationship to carry whatever conversations came out of our visit.

I was unsure of what even to do: shake Azim's hand with my own sweaty mitt, awkwardly nod in his direction or something else? After embracing my grandfather, I was saved by Azim who reached out to give me a hug. It was a hug that felt like he had been waiting to give for a long time. It was a hug that was empty of all the tension that I felt in my own chest; it was genuine. I felt silly and ashamed receiving something so sincere as a hug from a man who had every reason to hate me. I really enjoyed that first visit with Azim, even though I spent the entire visit feeling that "silly" and "ashamed" feeling that had settled on me.

Azim carried much of the conversation that day asking questions that were difficult, showing concern for how I was adjusting in prison (how the adult inmates were treating me) and what my goals were.

I mumbled through some answers, talking about my desire to go to school, my hopes of making something good out of my time (all the things that I thought were possible, but unlikely due to the dynamics of a maximum security prison). I was trying to sound both brave and purposeful without letting the doubt and uncertainty creep into my voice. I was as unsure of my future at that time, as a teenager could be, but how could I say that to this man I had taken so much from?

My impression of Azim, almost immediately was of a sincere human being. Our visit together confirmed to me both his sincerity and compassion. I know on some level that a person had to possess an immeasurable amount of personal strength to turn a life-altering blow like losing a child, into a commitment to address the issues of violence and forgiveness in our society, especially among our young people.

Azim seemed to me to be the strongest man that I had come across; his ability to forgive me in person after knowing the part that I played in his loss seemed supernatural. That day, and for a very long time after, I had trouble forgiving myself for my actions and felt unworthy of being forgiven by Azim or anyone else in my life.

Having the opportunity to meet Azim opened my eyes to the understanding, power and need for forgiveness in action. I had heard about forgiveness from a religious standpoint for most of my life. Since my incarceration I've read my share of cultural and individual ideas about forgiveness and its potential benefits, but I had, up until meeting Azim, never seen forgiveness in action up close before. I learned that forgiveness was a healing tool, where anger and revenge were stagnating emotions gnawing at the soul and diminishing the humanity of both the person enraged and the object of that rage. Forgiveness *is* empowering, freeing us from the resentment and the personal prison of our own pain.

Azim has been an underlining force in my life. He's offered a myriad of young people a pathway to understanding forgiveness, compassion and reconciliation. Having committed his life to sharing that understanding with the world, his message is an old one but one that is difficult to reconcile with the message of judgment and vengeance that crowds the forefront of our emotional pallets in "an eye for an eye" world.

Being the change that you wish to see in the world isn't easy by any means. But thanks to people like Azim Khamisa, there are examples that it's not impossible.

Tony Hicks
October 2013

Ples Felix, Tony Hicks and Azim Khamisa

INTRODUCTION

THE ROADMAP TO PEACE

Shortly after the 9/11 tragedy, when our country, as well as the entire world, was in a state of shock and fear, I emerged from a deep meditation with a profound "aha." I reached for my journal and wrote what I call a formula for peace:

Sustained goodwill creates friendship.

Sustained friendship creates trust.

Sustained trust creates empathy.

Sustained empathy creates compassion, and

Sustained compassion creates peace.

As I travel around the country speaking about peace and nonviolence, people continually ask me, "How do you extend goodwill to the person who killed your son?"

The answer is: "You do it through forgiveness."

"How do you forgive the person who killed your son?"

The answer is: "You do it through compassion and empathy."

"How do you have compassion and empathy for the person who killed your son?"

The answer is: "You must go beyond the physical, emotional and mental. You must get to your soul."

This book is the roadmap to the soul – the roadmap to peace.

From Fulfillment to Peace, my third book in a trilogy, is the culmination of a powerfully transformative journey that began on the morning of January 22, 1995. That was when I received a devastating call informing me that my only son Tariq had been shot and killed.

In my first book, *Azim's Bardo: From Murder to Forgiveness,* I describe in detail the tragedy that might have destroyed my life – had it not catapulted me onto a spiritual path that led to the creation of the Tariq Khamisa Foundation (TKF), a nonprofit organization dedicated to ending youth violence.

My second book, *From Forgiveness to Fulfillment,* describes how I found my way back to living a life filled with meaning and purpose.

I previously thought that this final book of the trilogy would be titled *From Fulfillment to Enlightenment.* But along my journey to enlightenment, something shifted. I found peace. I wasn't looking for peace. It simply came to me after enduring the loss of my son and transforming my grief into doing good deeds through compassion, empathy, and forgiveness. Such meaningful and purposeful work not only brought me fulfillment; it also gave me the gift of peace. People sometimes comment that I have a calm, peaceful, and gentle spirit. That's because even when things don't work out, I feel calm in my center. For this, I am in constant gratitude. So, if you, like me, are on a journey to enlightenment, you just might find a wonderful blessing along the way – the blessing of peace.

For me, peace is a stepping stone to enlightenment. Since I was able to achieve peace in the worst of circumstances, I believe that peace is achievable for all of us. I also have great conviction that we can get to peace quickly when we put it into daily practice. This book is about the process and practice of achieving and sustaining peace on both an individual and a global level.

As you read these pages, I have woven nuggets of spiritual wisdom to create a roadmap with detailed directions. It is my sincere wish that this roadmap will guide you to continually return to the high vibratory emotions that are essential to maintaining peace – no matter what happens in your life.

The true purpose of *From Fulfillment to Peace* is to provide practical strategies to help you shift negative emotions such as anger, jealousy, resentment, greed, avarice, gossip, and a myriad of other low vibratory emotions into high vibratory emotions such as goodwill, friendship, trust, empathy, compassion, forgiveness, love and peace – without having to become a monk, a saint or a recluse. We often think these emotions are "automatic." But believe me, they are not. I work hard at not losing my temper. From time to time I still get angry, but more often than not, I am able to preempt my emotional reaction – so I know that you can do it too.

Throughout this book you will find a blending of soulful wisdom from ancient and modern masters as well as examples of how to preempt those seemingly "automatic" triggers in your everyday life and stay in the higher vibrations of compassion, empathy and peace. Once you embody high-vibratory emotions and experience moments of bliss by learning to BE in these emotions, you will immediately know when you have "fallen off the wagon." Through introspection and meditation, you will better understand why you fall off the wagon. Then, with practice, you will fall off the wagon much less. As your awareness increases, you become more conscious of your state of being. Rather than reacting to external triggers, you can choose to radiate from a place of peace, which is your truest nature.

Most people would agree that losing a child to a senseless gang-related murder has to be one of the most difficult experiences to endure and overcome. They would also agree that finding peace with it would be a difficult challenge. Yet, through the insights and practices found in this book, I have found peace, my family has found peace, and Tony, the perpetrator, along with his family have found a sense of peace. On a more collective level, millions of children and adults who have been touched by the TKF story have found peace, too, as they arrived at a new understanding about creating, living, and being kind to themselves. Peace can have a resounding ripple effect from an overwhelming and shocking loss, so there is great hope and possibility that we can all find our way to peace. This is the greatest blessing.

I never set out to be a social change agent or a teacher of peace. For most of my life I was focused on the business of making money. Yet, out of the deep despair at the loss of my son, I discovered a much more meaningful path. I discovered a formula for peace – a roadmap to the soul – and it is with deep appreciation and sincere love that I share this peace formula with you so that you and your loved ones, our nation, and the entire world, may one day live in peace.

STRUCTURE

Each chapter in this book is based on the themes inherent in my Peace Formula. I have included a vast array of quotes from diverse religious scriptures to the greatest of luminaries and teachers of perennial wisdom. I selected these philosophies purposefully – with great care and intention – so that you, the reader, will have easy access to perspectives from the various scriptures as well as views on each topic from other wisdom traditions.

The quotes are universal; they come from all over the world, from all faiths, and from all wisdom traditions. After reflecting on these philosophies, I have interpreted them from my own point of view, based on my spiritual journey. My intention here is to demonstrate how I have managed to put these high universal concepts into practice along my journey to peace. I hope that you, too, will be able to do the same.

ONE SOUL

Irrespective of race, religion, color, nationality, socioeconomic status, age or gender, I continually return to the concept that there is one soul and we are all part of the same consciousness. I believe it is vitally important to awaken this awareness in everyone because part of achieving peace is to understand that we are all one – that there is no separation. The broader we can interpret the various scriptures, spiritual and wisdom traditions, the more we can see the common threads – that we really are all one. With this awareness coming alive in people's consciousnesses today, peace is permeating throughout the world. As more people start to think this way, the planet will undoubtedly shift in a major way.

Keep in mind that the soul predates the human race, going back to before the universe existed. The soul isn't black or brown or yellow or blue. It isn't young or old, rich or poor. It is our collective consciousness. We all come from one source – from one soul and from one consciousness. The world today is in its precise state of evolution because of our collective consciousness. But we have created all kinds of separation – from race to gender, from religion to nationality, to name a few. We've lost the understanding that we all come from one source. Instead, we've separated ourselves into Americans, Europeans, Israelis, Palestinians, black, brown, and white. Until we learn to respect everyone and acknowledge that we are not separate – that we are in fact the same and there are many paths to God – we will not have peace.

Even though I was raised as a Muslim, I have learned a great deal from the Christian faith, the Jewish faith, the Buddhist faith, the Hindu faith, and others. I have read books on all these faiths, and I see a lot of positivity in every one. So while you practice your particular faith, it is important to broaden your horizons and understand other wisdom traditions and faiths. Part of the mission of this book is to do just that – to share with you the commonality of some traditions and faiths so you can create and live according to the concept of Oneness within all of us.

I have always maintained the philosophy that I don't care what you believe, but I do care *that* you believe. This is because people with a strong positive belief system typically will espouse the higher values this book puts forth. You might believe in the sacred cow as the Hindus do or you might believe in Muhammad, Abraham, or Jesus, or in Universalism, New Thought or Scientology. The idea is that we have this potpourri of belief systems that makes the world very colorful – like a kaleidoscope. It is very rich.

MAYAN PROPHESY

For over 50 years, Joseph Robert Jochmans has been an avid researcher into the mysteries of both the past and future. He has been in pursuit of the forgotten wisdom of lost civilizations and the revelations of age-old prophecies from all corners of the globe.

He says, "Both the Hopis and Mayans recognize that we are approaching the end of a World Age... In both cases, however, the Hopi and Mayan elders do not prophesy that everything will come to an end. Rather, this is a time of transition from one World Age into another. The message they give concerns our making a choice of how we enter the future ahead. Our moving through with either resistance or acceptance will determine whether the transition will happen with cataclysmic changes or gradual peace and tranquility. The same theme can be found reflected in the prophecies of many other Native American visionaries from Black Elk to Sun Bear."

According to Mayan prophecy, by the end of 2012 we were on the cusp of the Mayan "end times," the end of a galactic day or time period spanning thousands of years. But in the Mayan structure of cyclic time and World Age transitions, our present cycle is as much about beginnings as it is about endings. Rather than being a linear end-point, the cycle that is ending will naturally be followed by the start of a new cycle. But what this new cycle has in store for humanity is a mystery that has yet to unfold.

Even though we have moved beyond the December 21, 2012 prophecy date, and no matter what is coming next, I feel this is a time of a monumental shift in which we are being ushered into a more enlightened age, one that is founded on our awakening to the beauty and responsibility of our oneness and interconnectedness. Carlos Barrios, trained as an Ajq'ij in the Maya tradition, says about upcoming changes:

"Our planet can be renewed or ravaged. Now is the time to awaken and take action...The prophesized changes are going to happen, but our attitude and actions determine how harsh or mild they are. This is a crucially important moment for humanity and for the earth. Each person is important. If you have incarnated into this era, you have spiritual work to do balancing the planet...The greatest wisdom is in simplicity. Love, respect, tolerance, sharing, gratitude, forgiveness. It's not complex or elaborate. The real knowledge is free. It's encoded in your DNA. All you need is within you. Great teachers have said that from the beginning. Find your heart, and you will find your way."

This book will guide each and every one of us (myself included) to stay connected and grounded to our oneness and that which is of the highest vibration. This simple yet profound wisdom is the foundation of my "Peace Formula" and the focus of this book.

Through daily practice, we can be better prepared to transition into this enlightened age. If we begin now, we will ensure an enlightened era because we will become part of the tipping point. If more of us can remain in the higher vibratory states described in this book, the shift will be easier to handle in transformative years to come.

Dr. David Hawkins, Director of The Institute for Advanced Theoretical Research, states: "*One individual who lives and vibrates at the level of peace counterbalances 10 million individuals who are living and vibrating at the lower levels of pride, anger, desire, fear, grief, apathy, guilt and shame.*"

With this book, I am thrilled to share more of the wonderful insights I have gathered along my 18-year journey, as I traveled from forgiveness to fulfillment to peace. I believe that together we can and we will create the formula for the enlightened era that we all envision.

Mankind must remember that peace

Is not God's gift to his creatures;

It is our gift to each other.

~ Elie Wiesel, Author, Holocaust survivor

CHAPTER ONE

FULFILLMENT

"One great question underlies our experience, whether we think about it consciously or not: What is the purpose of life? I believe that the purpose of life is to be happy. From the moment of birth, every human being wants happiness and does not want to suffer. From the very core of our being we simply desire contentment."

~ Dalai Lama, Tibetan spiritual and political leader

Throughout my life, I have been drawn to sacred texts, ancient spiritual wisdom, mystics, poets, and luminaries. I believe that without a direct experience, even the most sacred words are mere thoughts, ideas and concepts. And so, I have spent many moments in contemplation on the words of the greatest prophets, masters and gurus. Yet, it was not until tragedy and crisis visited me that I was able to fully comprehend and put into daily practice the profound truths that are scattered throughout this book. The last eighteen years of my soul's awakening journey – which began with the murder of my son and continues to this day – have served as a real-life example of how we can transform our darkest hours into our brightest glories and make the world a better and more fulfilling place for everyone.

The dictionary defines "fulfillment" as: "feeling satisfaction at having achieved one's desires." To me, it means something much more. I see fulfillment as the experience of your soul aligning with your life purpose and the work you do to create that alignment is a reflection of that. Rumi, a famous Persian poet and mystic, one of my favorites, said this: "When you do things from your soul you feel a river moving in you, a joy."

Rabbi Michael Berg, Translator of the Zohar, offers his insight: "It is the Light of the Creator we experience in those moments when joy overtakes us, or when beauty suddenly illuminates our lives."

George Bernard Shaw, Irish dramatist and socialist, offers another perspective:

"This is the true joy in life, being used for a purpose recognized by yourself as a mighty one. Being a force of nature instead of a feverish, selfish little clod of ailments and grievances, complaining that the world will not devote itself to making you happy. I am of the opinion that my life belongs to the whole community and as long as I live, it is my privilege to do for it what I can. I want to be thoroughly used up when I die, for the harder I work, the more I live. I rejoice in life for its own sake. Life is no brief candle to me. It is a sort of splendid torch which I have got hold of for the moment and I want to make it burn as brightly as possible before handing it on to future generations."

FINDING FULFILLMENT THROUGH WORK

I found fulfillment – the alignment of my soul and my life purpose – through the work of helping others as I chose a life of peace making, forgiveness, and freedom. This work, which I often refer to as "spiritual activism," grew out of my strong desire to heal from the despair and darkness following the loss of my son. By finding the ability to open my heart, by using the daily practice of forgiveness, and by sharing a story that helps others to heal, I continually find a sense of fulfillment I never dreamed possible. There are no words to describe my inner joy at knowing that I have touched another's life and helped him or her shift from pain to purpose. This is my deepest contentment.

Nobel Laureate in literature in 1913, Rabindranath Tagore, another favorite author of mine, was a Bengali mystic, poet, artist, playwright, novelist, and composer. Before the tragedy that took my son's life and put me on my spiritual path, I probably would not have understood what he meant when he said: "I slept and dreamt that life was joy. I awoke and saw that life was service. I acted and behold, service was joy."

I get it now. Joy, happiness, and fulfillment from a life of service were not part of my plan as an investment banker. But like a seed that grew within my heart and soul, fulfillment bloomed for me unexpectedly by practicing empathy, compassion, goodwill, and forgiveness. The decision to transform the tragedy that took my son from me placed me on a journey that infused great meaning and purpose into my life. As I have helped others in bringing more healing to their lives over the last eighteen years, I, in turn, have been blessed with more light, healing, and fulfillment in my own life.

I learned first-hand (the hard way) what Mahatma Gandhi meant when he said, "As human beings, our greatness lies not so much in being able to remake the world... as in being able to remake ourselves."

I was fortunate to be able to remake myself. I know that now, I am a better person than I was when Tariq was alive. As I have endeavored to connect with my higher power, and expand my consciousness, I have come to understand we are here to serve humanity. Through sharing my story, day after day, year after year, I watch kids and adults being transformed. Their hearts empathize with my loss and they are inspired by my forgiveness for and friendship with Tony's grandfather, Ples. As more and more people expand their consciousnesses and choose to embrace empathy, compassion and forgiveness, the planet is healing and the ripple effects are infinite.

Most fulfilling to me is hearing from students and adults who have been inspired, restored, and healed by hearing my story. To know I have lit another's candle by sharing my own flame is an indescribable blessing. One woman who recently attended my leadership seminar describes how she was inspired to become a supporter of the Tariq Khamisa Foundation:

"I believe that our children need to find a message of hope and peace in their lives. I had the privilege of hearing Azim speak at the Heart of the Samurai conference. My inner life has evolved from that point on. Someone asked Azim, ' How do we know what the right thing to do is when there are so many conflicting choices and emotions?' That was a core problem for me. I never knew what the right choice was and I worried and felt guilty over many decisions.

Azim said, 'If you can, ask your head, Is this reasonable? Then ask your heart, Does this feel right? Then ask your soul, Is this good? If you can answer yes to all three questions, then it is a good decision and your soul will be uplifted. If you say no to any one question, then it is not to be acted upon.'

After he said those words, my soul was uplifted and I felt a weight fly away from me and a peace descend upon me. At that moment, I knew I had been blessed with a revelation from God through Azim. It was life changing and has given me a firm foundation when I am faced with tough decisions. Azim gave me a precious gift and I want to reciprocate with my donations. I've experienced his powerful message first-hand and I believe he has the ability to reach many troubled children. Thank you Azim for your good work."

TRANSFORMATION: BRINGING LIGHT TO DARKNESS

"Though I sit in darkness, the Lord shall be a light to me."
~ Micah 7:8

Eighteen years ago, when I learned that Tariq had been shot and killed, I thought my life was over. How could I go on? How could I ever feel joy and happiness again?

This blinding moment of tragedy felt like a nuclear bomb detonating in my heart – something no human being, especially a parent, is prepared to endure.

Yet out of this intense anguish, darkness, and despair, I found light. In the Beatitudes in The New Testament, Jesus said, "Blessed are the pure of heart, for they shall see God." When the pain was too great to bear, I felt the life force drain out of my body, and I went into an altered state of consciousness. There, I felt held and comforted in the arms of my God. In that state of peace, I had a profound realization:

There were victims at both ends of the gun.

I knew it was true, but this was so far removed from a "normal" reaction to my son's murder, it seemed inconceivable to others. I believe my understanding that could only have come from the soul, dawned on me due to my strong spiritual foundation and my lifetime practice of meditation. From the moment the realization resonated in my heart, I have felt a light like a laser beam that is able to penetrate through any darkness. And that light continues to expand. From the revelation of seeing victims at both ends of the gun, my heart – blown to bits in pain and despair – felt blasted open to a new level of compassion, empathy, and understanding. I was literally no longer the same man.

I am inspired by the words of Khalil Gibran, Lebanese/American artist, poet, and writer, who said, "Your living is determined not so much by what life brings to you as by the attitude you bring to life; not so much by what happens to you as by the way your mind looks at what happens."

I turned to the teachings of my Islamic faith and realized that I could mourn for forty days, but excessive grieving would actually impede Tariq's soul journey. Therefore, my faith directed me to turn my grief into good deeds for the living – deeds that would *fuel* Tariq's soul's journey, not *hinder* it. One of my spiritual teachers reminded me that the quality of the rest of my life depended upon my reaction to my son's murder.

I knew that for a life to have quality it must have purpose. My faith renewed me and gave me a reason for living – to help Tariq's soul on its journey. To this end, I would work to stop children from killing each other. I would create the Tariq Khamisa Foundation, a nonprofit organization whose mission is to empower kids, save lives, and teach peace.

Patanjali, compiler of the Yoga Sutras, eloquently describes the profound transformation that I recognized happening in me – something so grand that it would lead me back to a life of joy, peace, and fulfillment:

"When you are inspired by some great purpose, some extraordinary project, all your thoughts break their bonds: Your mind transcends limitations, your consciousness expands in every direction, and you find yourself in a new, great, and wonderful world. Dormant forces, faculties, and talents become alive, and you discover yourself to be a greater person by far than you ever dreamed yourself to be."

So how do we bring a sense of purpose and fulfillment to our lives when we are faced with hurt, pain, anger, grief, sadness, loss, emptiness, depression, resentment, disappointment, judgment, and other destructive emotions? In my second book, *From Forgiveness to Fulfillment*, Tariq's sister Tasreen shared how she was able to find fulfillment following the devastating loss of her brother. Three years after the tragedy she moved to San Diego to work beside me as TKF's Assistant Executive Director. Within a year, she became our Executive Director and fell in love with what she was doing.

"It didn't feel like a job to me," she said. "I was doing my life's work in the name of my brother, which he wasn't able to finish in the physical world, and it felt good not to have the tragedy be in vain. Through his death, my brother gave my family a wake-up call to really look at our lives. He put us on the path to our life's work and the way we were going to contribute to the world. He connected me back to my soul again, and after my brother passed, I really got to start fulfilling what I thought my purpose in life was."

Albert Schweitzer, German/French theologian, musician, philosopher, physician, and Nobel Peace Prize winner, said, "I don't know what your destiny will be, but one thing I know: The only ones among you who will be truly happy are those who have sought and found how to serve." I can attest to this.

HIGH VIBRATION ~ LOW VIBRATION

There are two kinds of emotional reactions to any situation – high vibration and low vibration. One feels good and one feels bad. I like to remind people that we always have a choice as to our emotional reaction in any given situation – always.

I am speaking here from direct experience. Had I chosen to stay in the low vibratory emotions of anger, sadness, grief, and despair when I lost my son, I could have dipped into a depression so deep, I might have taken my own life. I was that close. Yet, because of my spiritual foundation, my meditation practice, and the support of my spiritual teachers and family, I experienced a deep soul awareness not based in logic.

When you are in this kind of deep pain, there comes a point when you have to decide whether you want to continue to feel bad or make a shift in how you perceive what has happened so you can begin to heal and feel good again. Ralph Waldo Emerson, American poet, lecturer, and essayist said, "The reason why the world lacks unity, and lies broken and in heaps, is because man is dis-united within himself."

Rather than staying in the negative emotions that would have debilitated me and destroyed my life, my soul showed me another way – one of compassion, empathy and understanding. It was this high vibratory choice that led to the most positive outcome for everyone involved. But it did not come from my intellect. Even after questioning and agonizing for months, my intellect provided me no solace, solution or direction. Instead, the solution came from my heart and soul.

Yes, I felt bereft and was filled with rage, but my anger was not aimed at Tony, the young man responsible for Tariq's death. In a flash, I saw what I previously mentioned – victims at both ends of the gun. Tariq and Tony were both victims of our violent society, one that I had been a part of shaping. What I didn't know at the time was how this horrible tragedy would be the catalyst for my spiritual awakening and my dedication to help bring solace and peace to many people, young and old, from all walks of life.

Words by Gautama Buddha, the founder of Buddhism, have much greater meaning in my life now: "Just as treasures are uncovered from the earth so virtue appears from good deeds, and wisdom appears from a pure and peaceful mind. To walk safely through the maze of human life, one needs the light of wisdom and the guidance of virtue."

FULFILLMENT = GRATITUDE

On January 21, 2013, my mom, my daughter Tasreen, Tariq's mother Almas and I had dinner together. It was the 18-year anniversary of Tariq's death and had it not been for TKF, it would have been a very difficult evening. With TKF in place, it was almost easy, because we could celebrate the incredible work being done in Tariq's name. So there wasn't the sadness that typically comes at the anniversary of this type of tragic event. There was instead a sense of fulfillment.

When Tariq was alive, I expect that I was just like anybody else. While I meditated an hour a day, I did not have the quality of peace I currently enjoy. How amazing it is that taking on and coming through the hard knocks of life can make you a more peaceful person! I know that tragedies can destroy you or they can make you better based on the choices you make. I thank the good Lord and my mother (who gave me a strong spiritual nature) that as a result of this tragedy, I am a better person.

You see, I didn't have this extraordinary sense of purpose and meaning when Tariq was alive. Now I really have a lot of both, and I'm grateful to Tariq for this blessing. I am reminded again of the poetic words of Khalil Gibran: "When you are joyous, look deep into your heart and you shall find it is only that which has given you sorrow that is giving you joy. When you are sorrowful look again in your heart, and you shall see that in truth you are weeping for that which has been your delight."

Through forgiveness, I have gone from being a tough investment banker to being a healer, a social worker, and a teacher of peace. I am able to visit my son's grave in gratitude, not grief. This is fulfillment. Thank you, Tariq, for your many blessings and for the wisdom that continues to speak to my soul.

STREAM OF LIFE

"The same stream of life that runs through my veins night and day runs through the world and dances in rhythmic measures. It is the same life that shoots in joy through the dust of the earth in numberless blades of grass and breaks into tumultuous waves of leaves and flowers. It is the same life that is rocked in the ocean-cradle of birth and of death, in ebb and in flow. I feel my limbs are made glorious by the touch of this world of life. And my pride is from the life-throb of ages dancing in my blood this moment."

~ Rabindranath Tagore, Bengali's mystic and poet Laureat

CHAPTER TWO

FORGIVENESS

Then Peter came to Jesus and asked, "Lord, how many times shall I forgive my brother when he sins against me? Up to seven times?" Jesus answered, "I tell you, not seven times, but seventy times seven."

~ Matthew 18:21-35

FORGIVING TONY AND REACHING OUT TO PLES

I am often asked what inspired me to forgive Tony, the boy who shot and killed my son, and what inspired me to reach out in forgiveness to Ples Felix, Tony's grandfather and guardian. My answer is that out of years of deep and long meditations, my soul directed me there.

It took a while, but five years after the tragedy, I met with Tony Hicks and told him that I held no animosity toward him. When Tony asked for my forgiveness, I granted it to him. People wonder what happens when you forgive somebody who has not asked for forgiveness? What I always tell them is that I forgave Tony long before he asked for my forgiveness. In fact, he thought that everybody in his life was stupid – his grandfather was stupid for disciplining him; Tariq was stupid because he wouldn't hand over the pizza; the D.A. was stupid because he didn't take care of him. Then something happened to him the day before the trial – and it clicked. This was when he figured out that the only person who was stupid was himself. This was when he took responsibility for killing Tariq – and then he asked for my forgiveness – which had already been granted.

I had spent a lot of time thinking about this. Mike Reynolds, the D.A., talked with Tony 22 times. Ples told him that the forgiveness was unconditional on my part – and that he needed to do the right thing. So now when people ask me that, I tell them, when you forgive somebody and they don't ask for forgiveness back, check the quality of your forgiveness. It has to be unconditional; it cannot have strings attached to it.

Ples Felix and Azim Khamisa

AUTHENTIC FORGIVENESS

Forgiveness is of the heart, not the mind. When you truly forgive, that is a selfless act, and it will create empathy. It may take some time like it did for me with Tony, but if your forgiveness is authentic, it will transform the other person.

People have said, "Well that's fine for you, Azim, because Tony asked you for forgiveness." But that isn't why I forgave him. I forgave him because I wanted to feel better and to be at peace in my own heart. And that quality of forgiveness changed him too.

In my forgiveness workshops, I am often asked, "What do you do about repetitive domestic abuse?" The answer is easy:

You must immediately remove yourself from any abuse. And at some point later, you can try to forgive them or you will remain a victim. Gautama Buddha, the founder of Buddhism, said this: "Holding on to anger is like grasping a hot coal with the intent of throwing it at someone else; you are the one who gets burned."

When I think of Tony, my blood pressure doesn't go up any more and my heart doesn't start to pound. He now has a safe passage through my head and my heart and if anything I get calmer because I have created a lot of love for him at the foundation.

The thing is that even when I first met Tony, I did not see a murderer in his eyes. I saw another soul just like me because we all come from the same source. That level of empathy is needed when you forgive without strings attached. I truly believe that when forgiveness is authentic, there's no way the other person will not shift.

But authentic forgiveness is not easy. It's a big job, a process that improves with practice. I forgive Tony every day, and he is in my thoughts a lot. But it's important to vibrate at that high level if you want to find peace. Mahatma Gandhi said, "The weak can never forgive. Forgiveness is the attribute of the strong."

A FORGIVENESS MUSCLE – BUILDING SYNAPSES

Once you get onto this path, you are essentially going to get better at it as you build and strengthen your forgiveness muscle. You do this by forgiving many little things on a daily basis. As a result of that, synapses actually connect in your brain and make forgiveness pathways that start to get more and more reinforced. The more you practice, the stronger these synapses get, and you'll be staying in that higher space for longer periods of time.

So my best advice is to get on the path and start practicing! Over the ensuing months and years, these synapses will get much stronger. I cannot emphasize enough the benefits of the guided forgiveness meditation on my website, offered as a free resource. The link is listed at the end of this chapter, so why not begin today? It is the quickest, surest, clearest path to building your forgiveness muscle and living from a space of peace.

When I forgave Tony, I saw two shifts take place in him. One happened eighteen months after the tragedy when he took responsibility at his trial. It was about nine months after I had reached out to Ples. But an even bigger shift arose in Tony five years later when he and I met.

At that time, I told him, "You've done something very wrong – you took a life of an innocent human being. It's tough on you too – I can tell. But I have forgiven you. Not only have I forgiven you. I've been working with your grandfather for a good four years now. I want you to know that when you come out, there's a job waiting for you at the Tariq Khamisa Foundation if you want to join us."

I created the space for Tony, and though he didn't have to step into it, this was a time period when he began to study for his GED. He ended up passing with flying colors.

During TKF's Violence Impact Assembly, when Ples speaks to the students, he explains how the opportunity that I gave Tony changed him. Ples says, "Most inmates have no hope. For the first five years, Tony thought he was going to die in prison. He had no hope. He was so afraid every time I visited him, he kept saying, 'I'm gonna die in prison, I'm gonna die in prison.'"

Ples goes on say that my offering him a job was the turning point. Most inmates don't have a job waiting for them but Tony does. That gave him so much hope that he began reading five books a month. He doesn't talk about dying in prison anymore. He's taking college courses now because he wants to help TKF after completing his prison sentence.

On my wall, I have a letter from a student that says, "The ultimate level of love is forgiveness." Even more amazing than forgiving is being able to say, "I see the pain in the person that hurt me too." Your forgiving them will help them, but they still may not feel good about themselves because they have done something horrible. Now it is your job, should you choose to accept it, to give them an opportunity to redeem themselves as your forgiveness turns into love. This is a very high form of forgiveness. It is one thing to give up all the resentment and touch somebody by saying, "I don't harbor any hard feelings by what you have done to me – I forgive you." But it's a different story altogether when you can say, "I'd like to now help you to redeem yourself."

"The Ultimate Level of Love is Forgiveness"

I have received tens of thousands of letters from students and adults who have been inspired by the TKF story and the forgiveness teachings. It brings me great joy to know that these inspired souls have found a place within themselves to forgive so they can find their way back to a life of fulfillment and peace.

THE ULTIMATE LIBERATOR

My reaction to my son's killer was my ultimate liberator. It was my path to becoming whole again and beginning my journey to fulfillment. Little did I know that it would lead me to a much deeper level of inner strength, freedom and peace. And still, there is a great deal of confusion and a lack of understanding about the importance of forgiveness. Many people sign up for abundance workshops, but forgiveness is a much harder sell. Yet, what most people don't realize is that forgiveness is the single most powerful process and practice that heals hurts and broken hearts, restores health and vitality and liberates us to ultimately remember and rejoice in our truest nature – peace, love and joy.

Restoring your health and vitality and being connected to your truest nature will ultimately lead to abundance. But abundance will be difficult if you are carrying around a lot of resentment. Most of us are either skin bags of resentment or skin bags of guilt. We have resentment towards people we don't even know, like someone who cuts us off on the freeway. We judge people every day because we stay in that resentment, or we feel guilty for something we have done – maybe to a family member or to somebody else.

Let's keep in mind that we all make mistakes and we are treated the way we treat others. Abundance is hard to achieve when you are stymied with your relentless feelings of resentment. But through forgiveness, you can free yourself and get to your truest nature. Good health and vitality are precursors to abundance, but only with authentic forgiveness can you release harmful emotions like resentment and guilt. Nelson Mandela, former President of South Africa and Nobel Peace prize winner, made this saying famous: "Resentment is like drinking poison and then hoping it will kill your enemies."

MEDITATION ~ A SPIRITUAL FOUNDATION

Without my meditation practice and a strong spiritual foundation, I could never have ended up where I am today. Thich Nhat Hanh, expatriate Vietnamese Zen Buddhist monk, teacher, author, poet and peace activist says, "Meditation is to have the time to sit down and to look deeply and when you look deeply, you begin to understand. The moment when you understand, compassion is born in your heart. And now it is possible for you to forgive...not before that."

There are many ways to develop a spiritual foundation. These include prayer, reading inspirational literature, music, nature, going on retreats, and journaling. I am not suggesting that one is better than the other, but for me, the most powerful is meditation. I would say that 90 percent of my spiritual practice is meditation. The other 10 percent is all the other stuff – I journal, read, pray, and practice forgiveness every morning.

I know for sure that meditation can be transformative. When Tariq died, my education in math and finance at several excellent universities and colleges in Great Britain were of little use to me. The problem with education is it develops only the intellect. And while developing the intellect is a good thing, it does not solve our most heartfelt problems. Albert Einstein's words ring very true for me when he said, "We should take care not to make the intellect our god; it has, of course, powerful muscles, but no personality. It cannot lead; it can only serve."

The mind can justify a lot. We've all done that. The extreme example is Hitler who justified killing six million Jews and many others. And every one of the people who worked with him also justified that decision in their minds. Most of these experts were doctors and PhDs who were trained to do the opposite: save lives, not take lives. It begs the question: How can anyone justify something like that? Perhaps they can because the mind on its own is limited and has the tendency to lead some in the wrong direction.

The mind by itself can be detrimental, if you rely on intellect alone. And a lot of people do. While I have great respect and admiration for those who have achieved PhDs, the point is that the solutions to my life's deepest crisis didn't arrive from intellectual knowledge, training or wisdom.

When you begin with intellect and you add emotion and spirituality (adding the heart and soul to the head), it becomes very powerful. Intellect reaches a whole new level when it transcends the mind and the heart. One of our greatest scientific thinkers, Einstein, eventually became more spiritual. He got to the point where he saw that the observer became the subject and he entered what he called "the empty space." Medical doctor and spiritualist, Deepak Chopra, says that when you look at a cell, it is mostly empty. But it is not empty because therein lies the soul.

If you are reading this book, you probably have some sort of spiritual foundation already. Those who are evolved generally spend time in their hearts, but the heart alone, just like the mind, is not necessarily reliable. We all get carried away with our emotions – myself included – because there is no rudder in the heart. By the way, I am not suggesting that a good mind and a feeling heart are not great assets, but they are not enough to deal with life's challenges. We must go beyond the mind and heart. We must connect with our higher self, our soul, our source.

CONNECTING WITH OUR HIGHER SELF

Meditation is one way you can connect with your higher self, your inner being, your soul, your source. It's a listening thing. This is listening to God. It is calling in our bullet proof spirit. It is where clarity resides. The soul is not going to justify that which doesn't make sense – like killing people. The soul doesn't get carried away like the heart does. It is in the soul that we find wisdom, resiliency, clarity, strength, warmth, compassion, safety, security, peace and love. The soul is grounded and pure. It always makes decisions that are in the highest good for you, the other person and the universe. The intellect is not grounded, and sometimes it is not pure because it knows how to justify. One of my good friends says the mind is a dangerous place to go by yourself.

The real irony is that everything that we require is already in the soul. I get a lot of my "ahas" as a result of meditation, but it is not easy for everybody. It works for me because I see the mind is a thought-making machine, which doesn't have an off switch. Therefore, I have studied many meditation practices. In the Sufi tradition, people practice a meditation using a mantra that consists of one of the 99 terms for God in the Quran. El Rahim is the most beneficent; El Rehman is the most merciful; Al Akbar means God is great. In the Indian religions, a mantra is a sound, syllable, word, or group of words that are considered capable of "creating spiritual transformation."

Wikipedia says, "For the authors of the Hindu scriptures of the Upanishads, the syllable Aum, itself constituting a mantra, represents Brahman, the godhead, as well as the whole of creation. Kūkai suggests that all sounds are the voice of the Dharmakaya Buddha — i.e. as in Hindu Upanishadic and Yogic thought, these sounds are manifestations of ultimate reality, in the sense of sound symbolism postulating that the vocal sounds of the mantra have inherent meaning independent of the understanding of the person uttering them."

Nevertheless, such understanding of what a mantra may symbolize or how it may function differs throughout the various traditions. And it also depends on the context in which it is written or sounded. In some instances there are multiple layers of symbolism associated with each sound, many of which are specific to particular schools of thought. For an example, the syllable "Aum" is central to both Hindu and Buddhist traditions. In Tibet, many Buddhists carve mantras into rocks as a form of meditation.

The Gayatri mantra is considered one of the most universal of all Hindu mantras, invoking the universal Brahman as the principle of knowledge and the illumination of the primordial Sun.

Aum Bhūr Bhuva Svaha

(Aum) Tat Savitur Varenyam

Bhargo Devasya Dhīmahi

Dhiyo Yo Nahah Prachodayāt, (Aum)

There are many types of meditation – Transcendental, Vipassana, and Buddhist to name a few. The meditation that I have created is Western-friendly, and many people tell me that they find it easy. In this form, there is no need for a mantra because it is a guided meditation. I also use the alternative nostril breathing, which is from pranayama yoga. The idea is that the breath can control the mind. When you are focused on your breathing, your mind is not producing any thoughts. The breath is like the reins of the mind. There is always a slight gap between inhale and exhale, but as you progress in your meditation practice, the goal is to create less of a gap – as in the bow of a cello which is so smooth that you cannot tell when it changes direction from up to down. You are continuously aware of your breath because your breath controls your mind. If there is even a tiny gap, a thought can creep in. This is called "circular breathing," where there is a smooth transition between inhale and exhale. Anytime during the meditation, if your mind is wandering, you can always go back to the breath technique found in my guided meditation.

To practice this meditation, please click on the link for the free guided meditation preamble on my website:

www.AzimKhamisa.com.

FINDING THE GAP

The goal of meditation is to get into "the gap," where there is no mantra and no thought. It can be a challenge since people typically go from one thought to the next to the next to the next. But the gap between two thoughts is like a micro-second. The best example I have read is in the *Tibetan Book of Living and Dying*.

It seems that after twenty years of meditation, a man tells his master, "I'm quitting meditation because I can't find the gap."

The master tells him, "You have the gap; you just need to elongate it."

Although you may not be aware of it, you can expand the gap, but keep in mind that even the most experienced meditators get only seconds in the gap. Half a second is a long time there, so it's not like you're going to have forty minutes in the gap. I don't know anybody who manages that. The idea is to meditate using a method where you can increase the probability to get more time in the gap. If you meditate twice a day, which is what I recommend, then there is a better chance that you will experience the gap.

I like to meditate three times a day, including before sleep, but I don't even try to get into the gap at night. Since my days are very long and busy with meetings and presentations, at night I want to process my thoughts. If you see your mind as a basket full of apples, think of every apple as a thought. Now you try to empty the basket but some of the apples actually creep back into the basket. Then you have to take them out a second time. Sometimes you have take them out a third and even a fourth time.

Actually, that's a good clue about what you need to work on. When thoughts keep coming, there's probably a need for forgiveness or resolution. At some point you want to have an empty basket and then, you can go to sleep and dream. Even in the dream state you will be processing and releasing unresolved issues. When I get up at 3 or 4 or 5 a.m., I sit up in bed and meditate for an hour. This is when I focus on being in the gap – my real goal. You don't have to do it that long nor do you have to get up at 3, 4 or 5 a.m. – I am simply sharing what I do.

When you meditate, it's a good idea to sit up and have a straight back. A point that could be added to my meditation preamble is this:

There is a space on which to focus – inside the heart in your body, the third eye, and then also outside of the body. When you meditate you go outside your body. Consciousness is both local and nonlocal; it's in you and outside of you. I recommend gently pointing your gaze upwards, like looking ahead, so you won't go to sleep. If you want to sleep, you can meditate with your gaze downwards.

When I meditate, if I am in my heart space, I keep my gaze down. Then I go into my third eye, which is a very powerful place, and I move my gaze upwards a little bit. Do what works for you, but please make sure your body is comfortable. The main objective is to get in the gap because God is there where you find your wisdom, compassion and clarity.

MEDITATION: MANIFESTING THE HIGHEST GOOD

My morning meditation is how I manifest my day. This is in the audio preamble found on my website. I use this time to look at everything I am planning to do that day and then I decide the outcome. Obviously the outcome has to be for the highest good, not only for you and the other person, but for the universe as well. God will not be involved with anything that is not totally pure, in integrity, sincere, and of the highest morals. So don't meditate on robbing a bank! Greed, jealousy and avarice in your outcomes are useless. An outcome like "I want to get this contract signed and make a million dollars" may not be in the interest of the other person. You want the outcome to be in the highest good for you, the other person, and the universe at large. It is important to state: "May the outcome be in the highest good for everyone involved and for the universe."

Often I get the outcomes I want, but sometimes I don't. This is when I have to accept that the outcome I got was for the highest good. We all have a little bit of an agenda. Abraham Lincoln used to say that we all have our own self-interest at heart. But he added that it is only human and we shouldn't blame anyone. The point is that we need to make sure that when we are being selfish and our outcomes don't unfold, we need to ask ourselves, "Was that outcome in the highest interest for all?"

If you're going to meditate twice a day – at night and the morning – then use half the morning meditation to get in the gap, and the second half to manifest your day. If you meditate at night, the idea is to process your day so when you wake up, you have more of a chance to get in the gap because you've already done the processing. You've slept, you've dreamt, and you have refrained from adding any new data, and so your mind is relatively clear. Then you can ask spirit to help you get through your day and create outcomes that are of the highest good for all.

In my second book, *From Forgiveness to Fulfillment,* I describe a three-step forgiveness process that has worked miracles in people's lives. Meditation is a vital part of this process and in building forgiveness muscles. I have been inspired to record a guided meditation as my gift to those individuals seeking to experience a deeper level of forgiveness that can be accessed through meditation. This is my gift to you…

To download my free guided audio meditation on forgiveness, go to my website at **www.AzimKhamisa.com**.

For your contemplation:

The *Bhagavad Gita,* a revered sacred scripture of Hinduism, was taught by Krishna whom the Hindus regarded as the supreme manifestation of the Lord Himself. He is referred to as Bhagavan – the divine one.

In the *Bhagavad Gita,* Karma Yoga is essentially doing one's duties in life according to dharma, without concern about results – a sort of constant sacrifice of action to the Supreme without thought of gain. In a more modern interpretation, it can be viewed as duty-bound deeds done without letting the nature of the result affect one's actions.

Krishna advocates Nishkam Karma (Selfless Action) as the ideal path to realize the Truth. Allocated work done without expectations, motives, or focus on outcome tends to purify the mind and gradually allows one to see the value of reason. These concepts are vividly described in the following verses.

"To action alone hast thou a right and never at all to its fruits; let not the fruits of action be thy motive; neither let there be in thee any attachment to inaction. With the body, with the mind, with the intellect, even merely with the senses, the Yogis perform action toward self-purification, having abandoned attachment. He who is disciplined in Yoga, having abandoned the fruit of action, attains steady peace... He who sees Me in all things, and sees all things in Me, he never becomes separated from Me, nor do I become separated from him. The one who has attained unity worships Me, who dwells in all beings. Whatever his station in life, the yogi abides in Me."

~ *Bhagavad Gita*

CHAPTER THREE

SELF-FORGIVENESS

"The kindest and most compassionate thing you can do for yourself and others is to forgive yourself."

~ Anonymous

This book was completed in 2010; it was in the process of being published. However, at that time, I knew intuitively that it was not truly ready for publication. Something was missing, but I did not know what it was. It had chapters on each of the steps, I thought, for a recipe for peace – goodwill, friendship, trust, empathy, compassion and forgiveness. Then in 2011, I received a message while meditating that told me the reason it was not ready. The book was missing a very important ingredient I had almost omitted, not only in the book but also my own life. It was a chapter on self-forgiveness.

Over time, I have learned we cannot get to peace simply by forgiving others; we must also forgive ourselves. Where forgiveness heals the harm another has caused, self-forgiveness releases and atones for the harm we have caused. Where resentment, hatred, anger and revenge can be released through forgiveness, the act of self-forgiveness releases guilt, shame and self-hatred. Because both guilt and resentment carry heartbreak that separate us from our happiness and peace, this chapter points the way for a truly peaceful individual, free from the harm not only perpetrated *on* them but also *by* them.

It took several years after I forgave the murderer of my son and reached out to his guardian and grandfather that I realized that for me to get to peace I also had to look at myself, as well as those actions that harmed others.

I had to look upon my own deep regret. Once I got on the path of forgiveness, it didn't take too long before I started to see my own foibles, mistakes, unresolved past and "stuff." It didn't take long before the path of forgiveness converged into the path of self-forgiveness. And surprising to me – and perhaps to you as you venture on this journey – I found the path of self-forgiveness harder to approach and then complete.

When we harm somebody, it can become a festering wound within us. Our minds and hearts are sometimes occupied 24/7 because of the guilt of unresolved harm that we caused another, whether we did it consciously or unconsciously. And as Aldous Huxley wrote in *Brave New World*, "Chronic remorse, as all the moralists are agreed, is a most undesirable sentiment. If you have behaved badly, repent, make what amends you can and address yourself to the task of behaving better next time. On no account brood over your wrongdoing. Rolling in the muck is not the best way of getting clean."

Our poor behaviors can play on our mind constantly; it can have us lose sleep, and it can create a festering wound that oftentimes becomes a large deterrent from us functioning in an effective way. We can't be living at 100 percent with such mental and emotional burdens, and therefore we do not experience deep peace, joy or happiness. What must transpire is a healing of the wound, a direct observation and acknowledgment of what we did to cause the harm, an act of apology or atonement, and then a commitment to change the behavior that created the harm in the first place. Once we do this, then peace is indeed possible.

A NEW CHAPTER

As I write this new chapter for the book, my mind flows into thoughts of the past I rarely reveal, but I feel it is important to share here for the sake of transparent communication and true healing.

I did not always live in the same city as my kids. I did not live in the same home as my children from 1980 on, even leaving the home city Seattle, Washington in 1981 after my divorce. Tasreen was nine and Tariq was seven. I would see my children four times a year, and they would spend summers with me in La Jolla, California. I would talk twice a week on the phone with them. I never went to Tariq's wrestling matches or tennis games, and neither did I go to Tasreen's sporting activities or important events. I was not really involved in their day-to-day lives, and when Tariq vacationed in Kenya – though I helped sponsor the trip – I received a heartbreaking card from him that said, "Dad, I wish you were here."

Messages like this were very hard to receive. And yet, I never thought Tariq would die before I did. Because of this unbearable loss, I went a very long time feeling guilty that I had not spent a lot of time with Tariq while he was growing up. Over the 20 years he was with us, those times together were few and far between. It took a long time for me to come to grips with this painful reality.

But somehow I had to find resolve. The way I was able to come to grips was to first forgive the boy who killed my son, reach out in forgiveness to Tony Hicks as well as his grandfather Ples Felix, and then create a foundation in Tariq's name that would help other children be free from a life of violence and gangs. But there was one more step I had to take, even though I didn't know I had to take it, in order to be free and to find peace. And that step was ... to forgive myself.

I was to take the four steps of "self-forgiveness," which I wish to share with you now:

1.   TAKE RESPONSIBILITY FOR YOUR ACTIONS.

2.   OFFER A STRONG AND SINCERE STATEMENT OF REMORSE, REGRET OR APOLOGY.

3. MAKE A COMMITMENT THAT YOU'VE CHANGED THAT BEHAVIOR FOREVER, AND GIVE SOMEONE PERMISSION TO CALL YOU ON IT IF YOU GO BACK TO THE OLD BEHAVIOR.

4. SUPPORT ANOTHER IN MAKING A SIMILAR EMPOWERING CHOICE, OR STOP AT LEAST ONE OTHER PERSON FROM MAKING THE SAME MISTAKE.

STEP 1 – RESPONSIBILITY

The first step in self-forgiveness: *"Take Responsibility for your Actions."*

There is an awesome quote from the late inspirational speaker and teacher Jim Rohn: "You must take personal responsibility. You cannot change the circumstances, the seasons, or the wind, but you can change yourself. That is something you have charge of."

We all make mistakes. Everyone is human. However, we don't always take responsibility for those mistakes. The tendency is to blame someone else. The process of self-forgiveness begins with taking full responsibility for all of our actions. This actually empowers us for the rest of our lives. In an exercise I present in the Forgiveness Workshop, I have participants consider an action they performed in their lives that brought harm to another. They then answer these questions:

- What happened when you harmed another? What actions did you take?

- What was the state of your emotions when you acted?

- What in your life brought you to this state of emotion?

- How were you still responsible for the actions you took?

A great example of someone taking full responsibility for his actions is Tony Hicks, during the murder trial in 1996 and ever since. In court, Tony said of his actions on that fateful night my son was murdered: "I shot and killed Tariq Khamisa, a person I did not know or who didn't do anything wrong to me." That is how his public statement started, and it set the foundation of absolute responsibility. Now, this wasn't his initial take on the subject when he was first arrested. For months and months, Tony told investigators and lawyers how it was the pizza man's fault since he didn't give up the pizzas. But by the date of the hearing – two years after the murder – Tony had a more mature interpretation.

Typically in a court hearing, an offender pleads "not guilty," which leads to a costly and painful court case where testimony upon testimony drags loved ones through the experience of recounting the tragedy. Since Tony took responsibility for his actions, he spared our families much pain and the City of San Diego a court case that would spend much taxpayer money.

In the CANEI program, which aims to reinstate offenders back into upstanding society members, we know that offenders are oftentimes victims themselves who need empathy for their pain. Even so, this doesn't let them off the hook for being responsible for any actions that created harm. It's OK to make a mistake, and make a poor choice, but it's not OK to avoid responsibility for your mistakes. We make sure those in the program know that blaming another will not free them or help anyone; we instead support them in embracing the power of responsibility.

In my own life, I have done my best to take responsibility for the harm I've caused. For I have made my share of mistakes. I have held a grudge with a family member that required my humility to let it go. I have told lies to a loved one and hurt her deeply. Because of this, I make sure now to be absolutely careful about what I say, refraining from even telling white lies, which can reinforce synapses in the brain and create guilt and deep inner wounds.

And as I have said previously, one of the bigger experiences of regret came when I realized I could have been with Tariq more when he was alive. I took responsibility by acknowledging that I did not choose to spend dedicated time with Tariq. I didn't make the time. The guilt comes in because the truth is I could have made more time, but I did not. I desperately wish that I made a different choice while he was alive. It wasn't anybody else's fault; it was mine.

STEP 2 – COMMUNICATE REMORSE

The second step in self-forgiveness: *"Offer a strong and sincere statement of remorse, regret or apology."*

The second step in your process of self-forgiveness is to offer a sincere apology or statement of regret to those you may have harmed. This takes humility, one of the most powerful qualities a person can hold. It will also take courage. This apology need not be person-to-person since some people we have harmed may be out of touch, unwilling and not ready to connect with us, or – as in the case of my son – no longer alive.

Humility will be a key. As it keeps us from getting defensive or trying to defend ourselves in anyway, it empowers us. As poet C.S. Lewis said, "Humility is not thinking less of yourself, it's thinking of yourself less."

During my Forgiveness Workshop, I have participants write out a letter to communicate with those they have harmed. It's a message of regret, as it actually holds the vital steps they are taking to forgive themselves. Participants are invited to address those they've harmed with responsibility for their action, a sincere statement of remorse, a commitment to change the behavior, and a desire to help others learn the same lesson they have.

It does not matter if the request for forgiveness is granted or not; what's important is to extend the hand of love, symbolically or in reality, to those we've harmed. We do it for another and the relationship in between, and yet we also do it for ourselves.

This second step was taken very powerfully by Tony during the court case mentioned earlier. In court, Tony said, "I pray to God that Mr. Khamisa will forgive me for the harm that I have caused him." I imagine that was very releasing for him, and it was definitely a gift to me. Though such humility and expressions of regret can help a soul, sometimes it's a process that will take time. I've seen this true in the life of Tony who still suffers from nightmares and night sweats resulting from the tragic experience from his side of the gun.

When I make a mistake or get into an argument that is my fault, I wish to very quickly – within 48 hours – resolve it by making an apology, opening up a space for resolution. Also during this time I meditate an extra 30 minutes to my normal practice of two hours a day. When we realize we have harmed someone, we are given the opportunity to have this particular part of our personality surface. In this way, we have a chance to resolve the issue, halt the guilt, mend the festering wound and then change the behavior.

For my own statement of regret, I have apologized to Tariq, heart to heart, for not being there for him during his formative years. I pray that he receives it on some level, and I believe in my heart that he does.

If the apology can be combined with some form of positive action that makes up for the harm, in a form of atonement, then you can present something – whether that is a physical object, a kind action, or a symbolic offering. I always want to atone by taking some meaningful action – giving flowers or a card, cooking a meal or sending a gift.

I know of one youngster from the CANEI program who took atonement to a new level. He changed his identity in a specific, purpose-driven way. He shifted his life from being a car thief who stole other people's property, into becoming a locksmith, helping others who have locked their keys in their car. Redemption is always available to all of us. We just have to be open and willing.

STEP 3 - COMMITMENT

The third step in self-forgiveness: *"Make a commitment that you've changed that behavior forever, and give someone permission to call you on it if you go back to the old behavior."*

The goal of this chapter is to find the ways to forgive yourself so you can be free of the guilt, shame and remorse within you, and then relocate that state of happiness and peace. This state will help you bring your best to your own life, with others at work, with family and with your circle of friends. With the third step, you are making a stand to change your behavior and then solicit help in making sure you keep that commitment.

Changing a behavior can be quite difficult. Your behavior can be caused by a habit that is beyond your conscious mind. For true change, you must first look at yourself deeply, and see how you do behave that does not work for you ... or others! This is not only difficult, but with so many barriers and blind spots, it may also be impossible. Because of this, you will need to honestly look at yourself and even ask help from others to point out your blind spots. You will also need a very sincere motivator, an incentive, the strong and powerful "why" you want to change in the first place. As stated by author William F. Scolavino, "The height of your accomplishments will equal the depth of your convictions."

With a deep purpose, and a personal incentive, changing a behavior can be accomplished. What I have made sure to do, in light of my regret over missing out on much of Tariq's life, is to make as much time as I can now with my dear Tasreen and her lovely children Shahin, Khalil and Miya. I'm spending more time with my grandkids than I did with my own kids, knowing how important it is to make time with those people I love the most.

The reason to change the behavior – besides reducing guilt and maximizing the higher vibratory states – is so you do not reoffend and continue the same patters that could cause more harm. If you do continue the behavior, then you really didn't mean the apology or truly request forgiveness. To say, "I'm sorry" and then continue the same behavior indicates you haven't really dealt with the issue on the deeper level.

Once you change the behavior and halt the habitual actions, then you become a better person, and you spend more time in the high vibratory emotions. You don't sink to the low vibratory emotions, such as guilt and remorse. Author Maxwell Maltz spoke of a key in changing our habitual behaviors: "The 'self-image' is the key to human personality and human behavior. Change the self-image and you change the personality and the behavior."

The first part of this third step in self-forgiveness is to make the commitment to change the hurtful behavior; the second part is to allow another to call you out when that commitment is broken.

In the past, I have personally enrolled my daughter and my friend Dan to take that role. And in times they've brought to my attention my own failings, I have seen that as a blessing and not as a criticism. I can see it this way because of my desire to change my behavior for the good of others and the progress of my soul.

STEP 4 – HELP ANOTHER

The fourth step in self-forgiveness: *"Support another in making a similar empowering choice, or stop at least one other person from making the same mistake."*

To truly know you have learned the lesson, it's important to pass it along to another. Teaching makes for great learning. In this step you help another in not making the same mistake you made.

This vital last step helps you in "giving back" to society in a helpful way, and in the process helps to transform you and your life. Restoration is yours. Innocence is yours, as you act in a way that demonstrates that level of giving and care. A bold stretch in your journey, this is an invitation for you to rise above the past and learn from it, ultimately leading you to apply and then teach lessons you have learned. A great opportunity awaits you here.

In the CANEI program, kids who have been offenders perform community service projects so they can contribute to society rather than take from it. In the exercise "Transforming the Experience" in the Forgiveness Workshop I have participants answer two questions:

1. What higher lessons do you believe you will gain from taking the steps in asking forgiveness and in helping another?

2. What practical action steps can you take in the near future to help another not make the same mistake you have made?

Tony, once again, is a good example of someone who is able to teach others to live a different type of life. Even from jail he's been able to teach – through his many written letters, the three hours of interview he granted, and the court speech we use in our school program. And once he's released from prison, Tony will join us at TKF to speak live before kids along with me, in order to touch even more lives, and help teens in making good, peaceful choices.

The way I've personally been able to take this fourth step is through my communication with other parents. At my speaking events, I routinely impart to parents two very important messages:

1. I have held so much regret that I didn't spend more time with Tariq.

2. If you have kids, make sure you spend more time with them!

In fact, there was one workshop where one man hadn't spoken with his son in 10 years. That was the workshop where I inspired the man to reach out that very day, using my cell phone, in order to get hold of his son and close the gap. And so he did. For this man, for you, for me, and for all of us, we are given ample opportunities to close the gaps of resentment, guilt and shame. It starts with a choice, and then the application of a few steps along the path of peace and self-forgiveness.

A LOOK BACK

Now, as I look back with a more expansive perspective, I see I would not be doing any of this forgiveness and self-forgiveness work (for myself or others) had it not been for Tariq, for my lack of attention with him and for my loss. I feel inspired every day to reach out to the children and youth of our world in Tariq's name and help them make the good choice of nonviolence – with goodwill, empathy, compassion, forgiveness and peacemaking.

As I look back, it's amazing to consider that I am closer to Tariq now than when he was alive, since he is now with me always. Now, as I do the speaking events with TKF, I ask him, "Are you ready to speak with the kids?" I repeat his name many times a day. I have placed Tariq's photo on his altar where I always say goodnight to him as I am making my chamomile tea before retiring to bed and good morning when I make my English breakfast tea.

Often when I am home and eat alone, I will light a candle and put his photo on the dining room table and tell him what is going on at TKF, in my life and with the grandkids. Though these are things he probably already knows, it still feels good for me to share those happy moments, always in gratitude to him and the work I do in his name. It's part of my attempt to be with a son I missed for so many years, even when he was alive.

These recollections remind me of a story concerning Yoko Ono, the wife of slain musician John Lennon. A journalist spoke to Yoko back when John was murdered, saying "Your loss must be so hard since you and John were together 95 percent of the time." She replied, "Now I'm with him 100 percent of the time."

I may not be with my son in a physical way, but I am with him in a spiritual way. And that, as I happen to write this on the auspicious occasion of what would be his 39th birthday – because of the self-forgiveness work and all the work done by TKF in his name – it will be enough.

It took self-forgiveness to get here. I now recognize that self-forgiveness is such a vital part of the journey to find peace. It's one thing to forgive the people who have harmed you, but it's equally important to forgive yourself for harm that you caused. This chapter was all about facing the festering wound, dealing with what haunts you in guilt, and finding the path of redemption – through the four steps – so that you can live your life at 100 percent effectiveness.

As I write this book, I am learning that as I exist in a space of forgiveness and non-judgment, I can live in a world of higher vibrations. I'm learning that I never can let any argument or disagreement go unresolved for more than 24 hours. If something happens that is my fault I'm very quick to work to heal that. And when it's not my fault I offer forgiveness and support.

When I do these things, when I'm on that path, I'm able to come back to vibrate at the high vibratory emotions mentioned throughout this book. I do not stay down in the lower vibratory state of anger, resentment, greed, avarice and jealousy. I have found that when I start forgiving others in my life, I also become more self-forgiving. These are the two sides of same coin – one side of the coin is the resentment and the other is the guilt. And it's through taking responsibility, through humility, through the commitment to changing behavior, and through the act of atonement that we can ultimately come home to that haven of peace.

It's this peaceful state where we can work at our zenith at our job, relate with love in our relationships and live at our best in our lives. Our society is facing so many issues – gangs, violence, gun murders – and I believe we must do something about that, as we have come into the world to make it a better place for our children and our grandchildren. If we aren't out in the world living at 100 percent we can't make positive change and create a better world. Too many of us are not playing at 100 percent. My wish is that more and more of us – all of you reading these words now – will do the work of self-forgiveness and forgiveness so that the path from fulfillment to peace is followed, and the positive changes in the world can truly come – within you, all of us, and our peaceful world.

CHAPTER FOUR

GOODWILL

Sustained goodwill creates friendship.

~ Azim Khamisa, The Peace Formula

Nelson Mandela was the first man to be elected President of South Africa in a fully representative democratic election. He held the office from 1994–1999 after serving 27 years in prison for his leadership role in the movement against apartheid. Following his release from prison in 1990, Mandela supported reconciliation and negotiation, as he helped lead the transition towards multi-racial democracy in South Africa.

Since the end of apartheid, many have praised Mandela, including some of his former opponents. He has received more than one hundred awards over four decades, most notably the Nobel Peace Prize in 1993. Mandela said, "If you want to make peace with your enemy, you have to work with your enemy. Then he becomes your partner."

My good friend Dr. Sayyid M. Syeed is the National Director of the Islamic Society of North America. When I asked him what Islam says about goodwill, he responded, "The Prophet of Islam taught his religion, Islam for 23 years, its beliefs, its rites and prayers and virtues."

Someone once asked him if he could summarize faith in a sentence. The Prophet said, "Well, faith is your goodwill towards your creator, towards the Prophet of God and towards the people around you."

On February 5, 2009, President Barak Obama addressed former British Prime Minister Tony Blair, Vice President Joe Biden, members of his Cabinet, members of Congress, clergy, friends, and international dignitaries at the National Prayer Breakfast. He talked about goodwill and the one law that binds all great religions together...

"Jesus told us to 'love thy neighbor as thyself.'

"The Torah commands, 'That which is hateful to you, do not do to your fellow.'

"In Islam, there is a hadith that reads, 'None of you truly believes until he wishes for his brother what he wishes for himself.'

"The same is true for Buddhists and Hindus, for followers of Confucius, and for humanists. It is, of course, the Golden Rule – the call to love one another; to understand one another; to treat with dignity and respect those with whom we share a brief moment on this earth."

It is an ancient rule, a simple rule, but also one of the most challenging. For it asks each of us to take some measure of responsibility for the wellbeing of people we may not know or worship with or agree with on every issue. Sometimes it asks us to reconcile with bitter enemies or resolve ancient hatreds, and that requires a living, breathing, active faith. It requires us to not only believe, but to do – to give something of ourselves for the benefit of others and the betterment of our world.

CONNECTING WITH YOUR SOUL

In my experience, I have found the soul to be stronger and wiser than the head (intellect) or the heart (emotion). But many of us live only in our heads and our hearts a great deal of the time. There are many highly intelligent people with PhDs who have developed their intellect through education.

There are many brilliant artists who live in their hearts and can beautifully express their creativity. But it is only through the soul that we get our epiphanies and "aha" moments. When I learned of my son's murder, the understanding that there were victims at both ends of the gun did not come from my head or my heart – for the head and the heart are not capable of that kind of awareness.

Luke 2.14 in the New Testament proclaims, "Glory to God in the highest, and on earth peace, goodwill toward men."

Understanding that the soul is at the root of our most powerful strength and inner wisdom behooves us to tap into it. Only by transcending the head and heart and digging deeper into the soul can we truly experience the brilliance of such mystical poets as Rumi, Gibran, Hafez and others who are sprinkled throughout this book. I find these writings helpful in addition to my spiritual practice of meditation in staying centered, connected, and anchored in my soul.

Hafez, a Sufi mystic and one of the most celebrated Persian lyric poets, is often described as a poet's poet. His "Divan" (mystical poetry) is found at the home of most Iranians who recite his poems by heart. His life and poetry have influenced the course of post-fourteenth century Persian lyrics more than anyone else has.

In his poem, *Elegance,* Hafez says: "It is not easy to stop thinking ill of others. Usually one must enter into a friendship with a person who has accomplished that great feat himself. Then something might start to rub off on you of that true elegance."

ANCHORED IN YOUR SOUL

Spirit, divine wisdom, sacred essence, God, source, higher self – these words describe that which is of the soul. Just as there are many spiritual paths, there are numerous ways to connect with your soul.

But one thing is the same: To live from your soul takes practice – daily practice. To live *for* the highest good, we must live *from* the source of our highest good. We must stay centered, connected, and anchored in our souls. This takes three qualities: awareness, intention and practice.

Countless wise teachers have said, "We are spiritual beings having a human experience." Yet, since we have a human body and mind, we often forget who we really are. Without awareness, intention, and practice, we can easily forget our spiritual essence as we hurry through our days. We can become unconscious and stressed out as events transpire that seem out of our control. We may feel empty and uninspired, quick to anger or judgment. To remain anchored in our souls, we must remember:

• **Awareness** is being mindful and conscious of thoughts, words and actions.

• **Intention** is being soul-centered in thoughts, words and actions.

• **Practice** is shining our light through empathy, compassion, giving, and doing that which brings forth joy, inner peace and love.

PRACTICING GOODWILL

The idea that "sustained goodwill creates friendship" is pretty obvious, but how often do we see this in practice? We make friends by extending goodwill, so we're not going to make friends with another country by bombing them. Rather, we're going to create more enemies. Albert Einstein said, "Nothing that I can do will change the structure of the universe. But maybe, by raising my voice I can help the greatest of all causes – goodwill among men and peace on earth."

Think about how many really good friends you have. I can count my best friends on one hand – the people who have loved me through thick and thin, right and wrong, without judgment. They've just always been there, extending goodwill to me at various points in my life, and I have done the same for them. We all get hard hits in life. When goodwill is extended over the years, this goodwill remains between friends. Two of my very close friends from my school days in England whom I hardly ever see, come to mind. Even after years of not seeing one another, it takes about a half hour to catch up and we're back to our friendship. This is because true friendship survives.

We all go through misunderstandings with friends and relatives. But when conflict, disagreement, talking behind backs, or hurt feelings happen, it is essential that we continue to extend goodwill. When you compare how it feels to be around people who extend goodwill with how it feels to be around those who do not, you will see that goodwill carries with it the highest of vibrations. It is the essential foundation for leading a peaceful, fulfilling life, not only with our best friends, but also with everyone we encounter. If you can extend goodwill to every person you meet, you will free yourself from low vibratory emotions that are so destructive to your wellbeing.

GOODWILL – NO MATTER WHAT

A few years ago, I hired a marketing consultant to help me promote my message of non-violence through my workshops and books. I gave this man a few names to contact but to my surprise, one of my good friends, whom I'll call Paula, was totally offended by the call. She said to my marketing consultant, "How dare Azim give you my phone number. If he needs my help, he should call me himself."

Several weeks later, I received an angry letter from Paula, stating that she didn't appreciate my giving her phone number to my assistant. I immediately called her back and said, "I'm really sorry. I had no right to give out your number. I should have asked for your permission first. I haven't seen you in a long time and we're overdue for a get-together. Please accept my apology. You're like a sister to me. Let's get together and catch up. I'm happy to treat you to coffee or lunch."

I e-mailed her as well, and I was stunned to receive this e-mail in response:

"The problem with you, Azim, is that you live in an Azim's world."

I felt my anger rising. "How dare she" I thought. And then I reminded myself, "Khamisa, you can't go there."

Although I could feel the anger rising in me, I was able to preempt it before it took me over. I called my friend back and left a message. "Thank you, Paula," I said. "Thank you for telling me your truth. If you hadn't, I would never have known. You've done me a big favor, and I'm going to start meditating and working on it. I really want you to know how much you've helped me. I love you, and I still want to get together with you for coffee or lunch. Please call or e-mail me whenever it's convenient."

In less than an hour, I got a call back from Paula, saying, "I love you too, Azim."

By continuing to extend goodwill, we create and maintain friendships, not by revenge, attack or and bombs.

There is a quote I love from *A Course in Miracles*:

"The holiest of all spots on earth is where an ancient hatred has become a present love... What hatred has been released to love becomes the brightest light in Heaven's radiance. And all of the lights in Heaven grow brighter, in gratitude for what has been restored."

A Course in Miracles focuses on cultivating awareness of love in the self and in others. It teaches us that the physical universe and our individual self is a dream of separation, guilt and fear that resulted from our judgment against our reality of Oneness in the unity of God. Everything that seems to be external is entirely within our minds. However, when we allow our minds to be guided by the Holy Spirit (our memory of that Oneness), the world becomes our classroom to learn and practice forgiveness. This will undo our illusion of separation and allow the experience of Oneness and inner peace to return to our awareness.

GOODWILL IN BUSINESS

The American way of doing business is to move very quickly. That's why we need so many lawyers! I have spent over 35 years as an investment banker, and I am intimately familiar with the barrage of e-mails, phone calls, and signed agreements before new business associates, customers or strategic partners even meet. Is it any wonder, then, that they fail to find agreement and need to bring in lawyers? The problem is that they never got to know each other at a deep level before they began to work together. Therefore, they never created any goodwill and there was never any trust. In the absence of trust, those types of non-agreements inevitably fall apart.

E-mails and phone calls are of the intellect, not the soul. If we want to establish a solid long-lasting relationship, we must meet in person so we can really get to know one another. I don't know about you, but I find it very difficult to read someone's energy and get to know someone through e-mails and phone calls. But have you noticed feeling a physical energy when you meet someone in person? You can walk into a crowded room and be attracted to certain people's energies while at the same time you are repelled by others – even before you get to know them. This is not an experience of the head or the heart. Rather, it is an inner intuitive sense that is of the soul.

When I do business in Mexico, India, or in other third world countries, I notice how different it is. My business associates in these countries invite me to their homes, introduce me to their families. We get to know one another, and we see how the other treats his wife and children. A deep sense of trust develops and from there, we do our business dealings and make solid, lasting agreements.

These types of agreements don't fall apart after we've taken the time and energy to get to know one another. We are not "getting into bed with strange bedfellows," as the saying goes. On the other hand, when we rush to do business quickly, agreements can easily fall apart because nobody took the time to do the goodwill part – to get to know each other. The bottom line in business is that people don't invest in you until they trust you, so it is extremely important to develop a high level of trust. This kind of trust takes time to build, but the ensuing business deals are more secure and long-lasting.

This principle works the same with friends. When a good friend is no longer a friend, you'll see a lot of ill will there. But despite the ill will being projected in our direction, we have to train ourselves to avoid falling into this trap as we remember to live in the higher vibratory emotions. Only there can we find happiness. Philosopher and theologian Saint Augustine said, "To seek the highest good is to live well."

HAPPINESS IS A SPIRITUAL CONCEPT

Happiness is a high vibratory concept. Sure, we all have "bad hair" days, but whenever we fall off the high vibration wagon, we have to stand up and get right back on, remembering to extend goodwill.

The terrorist attacks on 9/11 provided a perfect opportunity to practice this. We had a unifying opportunity, but our government decided to drop bombs and we may have created more terrorists through these actions. We often do this in our own lives as we add more fuel to the fire, creating more of the very thing we don't want.

One of our biggest obstacles is that people are often eager to support ill will. If you get angry at somebody who treated you badly and you express ill will toward that person, the tendency is for your friends and family to support you by taking your side. Their intentions may be good, but there are no sides and they are unknowingly adding fuel to the fire. In fact, this kind of support is very dangerous. Siddhartha Gautama, founder of Buddhism said, "Whatever words we utter should be chosen with care for people will hear them and be influenced by them for good or ill."

I never support ill will from my friends or family because I believe I can turn it around by extending goodwill. You can do this, too, but first you will need to develop more compassion and empathy as you spend some time reflecting more deeply on why you may have attracted ill will in the first place.

IT'S NOT ABOUT YOU

In his bestselling book, *The Four Agreements,* author Don Miguel Ruiz offers great insight with his Second Agreement "Don't take anything personally." He writes, "Nothing others do is because of you. What others say and do is a projection of their own reality, their own dream. When you are immune to the opinions and actions of others, you won't be the victim of needless suffering."

A friend of mine, Alicia, who was about to be married, felt rejected by her in-laws. She was from a different heritage and ethnic background than the family she was marrying into, and she felt excluded and that she was being treated badly. This went on for a long time, and when nothing changed, she stopped attending family functions.

One day, Alicia called and told me about her feelings. She was understandably upset, and I said to her, "You can dim your light and respond with the same kind of darkness they are putting out, or you can shine your light. If someone doesn't have you on their birthday or Christmas gift list, you can still send them a birthday or Christmas present. You can continue to be loving because that's who you are. If you act against your own nature, how will that make you feel?"

I went on to reassure Alicia that her in-law's behavior actually had nothing to do with her. It was all about them. She said she felt better because she realized that it had nothing to do with her and she remained free to make her own choices.

The truth is, it is never about you. When you let someone wield this kind of control over you, you give them the power to extinguish your light. Why would you give someone permission to have that degree of impact on you?

Alicia now says, "I had to get to a place of empathy and compassion. I was blaming my in-laws because I felt they were blaming me for everything. But once I put myself in their shoes, I could see how hard it must've been for them and I was able to forgive. I realized that ultimately, people treat you badly when they're hurting inside. Once I found my empathy, I also found peace, and I saw that my in-laws needed love as much as I did. Once I began giving love, empathy, compassion, and understanding, everything shifted. This brought a lot of peace to all of us."

Six months later this relationship totally shifted, and Alicia and her in-laws consider themselves family.

Carole King, one of the all-time great songwriters, says in her song *You've Got a Friend:*

"People can be so cold. They'll hurt you and desert you. They'll take your soul if you let them. Oh yeah, but don't you let them."

A wonderful poem, *A Persian Rosary of Nineteen Pearls,* written by Mizra Ahmend Sohrab, a Persian-American author and Bahá'í, illustrates the highest vibration of goodwill towards all.

"Love and serve humanity. Praise every soul. If you cannot praise him, let him pass out of your life. Dare, dare and then ... dare more. Be original. Be inventive. Do not imitate. Be yourself. Know yourself. Stand on your own ground. Do not lean on the borrowed staffs of others. Think your own thoughts. There is no saint without a past. There is no sinner without a future. See God and good in every face. All the perfections and virtues of the Deity are hidden in you. Reveal them. The Saviour is also in you. Let His Grace emancipate you. Be cheerful. Be courteous. Be a dynamo of irrepressible happiness. Assist everyone. Let your life be like unto a rose; though silent it speaks in the language of fragrance. You are a trinity of body, mind and soul. The food of the soul is Divine Love Therefore feed your soul on Divine Love – so that the body and the mind be invigorated. Be deaf and dumb concerning the faults of others. Do not listen to gossip. Silence is the tale-bearer with lofty conversation. Never argue with any soul concerning his religious beliefs."

President Abraham Lincoln stressed that we all act in our own self-interest. It is part of being a human being, as this behavior is in our DNA. Therefore we must refrain from judging people – something we do automatically – when they act in their self-interest, especially when their actions feel like a personal affront. A better response would be to extend goodwill.

A look at Lincoln's biography will reveal that he was known for hiring his enemies to work with him by offering Cabinet positions to those opposed to his ideas. When his supporters took him to task about this, he said he felt that these people were not necessarily opposing him. Rather, he saw them as looking after their own self-interests. He found nothing wrong with that, because he recognized these actions as the way people protect themselves and survive. Instead of judging, Lincoln chose to extend goodwill, softening their differences and accentuating their commonalities.

Am I not destroying my enemies when I make friends of them?
~ Abraham Lincoln

CHAPTER FIVE

FRIENDSHIP

Sustained friendship creates trust.

~ Azim Khamisa, The Peace Formula

When it comes to the topic of friendship, masterful insights abound from authors, poets, and businessmen, as well as from a variety of religious and spiritual scriptures. Paramahansa Yogananda was an Indian yogi and guru who introduced many westerners to the teachings of meditation and Kriya Yoga. In his book, *Autobiography of a Yogi,* he stated, "There is a magnet in your heart that will attract true friends. That magnet is unselfishness, thinking of others first... when you learn to live for others, they will live for you."

B. C. Forbes, Scottish financial journalist/author who founded Forbes Magazine said, "The way to make a true friend is to be one. Friendship implies loyalty, esteem, cordiality, sympathy, affection, readiness to aid, to help, to stick, to fight for, if need be. Radiate friendship and it will return sevenfold."

Aristotle, the Greek philosopher and one of the most important founding figures in Western philosophy said, "We should behave to our friends as we would wish our friends to behave to us."

THE IMPORTANCE OF DEEP FRIENDSHIPS

While we all have a variety of acquaintances, most of us probably have a limited number of deeper friendships.

Sirach 9:10, from the Septuagint, states, "Forsake not an old friend; for the new is not comparable to him: a new friend is as new wine; when it is old, thou shall drink it with pleasure."

This quote, taken from the Greek version of the Hebrew Bible, always reminds me of my good friend Shamsher whom I met in high school. We both married girls named Almas. He was in my wedding, and I was in his. Although I spent most of my life in the US and we didn't see each other very often, after Tariq died, I went and stayed with him and his wife and their two kids in Dar es Saalam. They had a boy and a girl about the same time I had a boy and a girl, and we reconnected immediately.

I got so much strength from Shamsher after Tariq died, I decided I wanted to get an elephant hair bracelet, which is considered a good luck charm in Kenya. Since I don't support the poaching and killing of animals for products, I decided to create the bracelet in the same design, but made of gold. When I told Shamsher what I wanted, he referred me to a jeweler friend of his, and I explained to him what I had in mind.

When I got the call that it was ready, I was excited to pick it up. I expected it to be expensive since I had ordered it in 22 carat gold, and I was ready to pay for it. But when I tried to write a check, Shamsher had already paid for it the day before. Even though he has passed away, his friendship remains eternal for me. I am reminded of a quote by John Muir, American naturalist, author, and early advocate of preservation of U.S. wilderness. He said, "I am learning to live close to the lives of my friends without ever seeing them. No miles of any measurement can separate your soul from mine."

Alan is another close friend whom I met when I was 15 years old, and we have remained good friends for the last 35 years. I trust Alan so implicitly, I leave money in his English bank account since foreigners are not allowed to open a bank account there. When Alan's mother died, I knew that Alan was an atheist and would not be offering prayers for her. As a Muslim, we have a ritual where you offer a small tithe and special prayers are recited for the dead. I set this up for Alan's mom, since he couldn't, and he was happy about that.

Finally, Nizar is another of my dear friends who also lives in England. We don't get to see each other a lot, but Nizar was a mentor to me. He and I can talk for hours on end about one subject since we love to dissect thoughts and ideas. We break it down into very fine pieces and then we build it back up again, often staying up until 3 or 4 a.m. Nizar is married to a girl, Yasmin, from my hometown; she is also a close and trusted friend. All three of us have always shared a wonderful friendship. As a result, it doesn't take very long for us to reconnect when we do see each other. This year, I am making a commitment to go to England to spend time with both Nizar and Alan. I would do anything for them, and they would do the same for me.

Another one of my close friend who lives in San Diego is Dan. I met him as a client and we bonded immediately. We both feel that we may have been brothers in a previous life. Dan is 10 years my senior and a wonderful friend, mentor and role model. We both enjoy meditation and are active and like to work out. We get together not as often as I would like, as we both have very busy lives. We usually will go for a 4-mile hike and sometime at the end, stop for a glass of wine. It never takes us long to connect. We enjoy a deep level of trust and respect for each other. Whenever I have a difficult decision to make, I will brainstorm it with Dan. He has a brilliant mind and great values.

So how do we create these kinds of friendships? And, more importantly, if you don't have close friends who can weather anything, you may want to ask yourself why not. Ralph Waldo Emerson, American essayist, philosopher and poet, said, "The only way to have a friend is to be one."

Proverbs 17:17 in the Bible states, "A friend loveth at all times." When a friend of mine was going through a divorce, I expressed my feelings to him and told him that I would be on his wife's side. "You're going to treat her right, aren't you?" I asked him. He was shocked, but after I explained how I felt, that I wanted him to treat her kindly and generously, our friendship became deeper and his divorce became more harmonious. I knew how important that was since my wife and I were so harmonious during our divorce, we hired only one lawyer for the two of us. I remember the judge looking at us and saying, "You two get along pretty good. Are you sure you want to divorce?" He was surprised to see the grace and trust between us, and we continue to this day to enjoy a healthy and friendly relationship.

If you have wonderful friendships, take a look at how and why you developed them. Not that they are ever perfect. Nobody and nothing is perfect. There is a Turkish proverb that states, "Who seeks a faultless friend remains friendless."

We all have issues. But it is important that you develop the ability to create deep friendships. I really believe you never part from your true friends. They may not be there physically, but they are always with you on the emotional and spiritual planes. Right now as I am writing about my friends, I am connecting to them – even to my friend Shamsher who has passed away. I am drawn to one of my favorite passages from Khalil Gibran's beautiful book, *The Prophet*. He writes, "When you part from your friend, you grieve not; for that which you love most in him may be clearer in his absence, as the mountain to the climber is clearer from the plain."

I believe that when you're with your friend, you really don't understand his or her majesty because it's like being a mountain climber. When you're climbing the mountain, although you can't see it beneath you, it can be seen from a distance. In the same way, when you leave a friend, the majesty that the two of you share is always there. So when I think of my friends from afar, I can see their majesty first.

Do you have friends like mine? If you do, ask yourself, what were the elements in place that enabled you to create those friendships? You will see that sometimes your friends have deceived you, haven't paid back a money loan, and sometimes brought up other relationship issues. But you are still friends, first and foremost.

There is an Arabian Proverb that states, "A friend is one to whom one may pour out all the contents of one's heart, chaff and grain together, knowing that the gentlest of hands will take and sift it, keep what is worth keeping and with a breath of kindness blow the rest away."

In spite of tough times that we all go through, I have found that true friendship transcends all difficulties, as you remain connected with no separation. I often talk about Tony and me not being separate, which may be hard for people to comprehend because of the circumstance. But learning to develop that quality of friendship with your truest friends – in spite of anything – is extremely important. Greek Philosopher Epicurus said, "Of all the means which wisdom turns to in order to ensure happiness during all our life, by far the most important is friendship."

The Dalai Lama, Tibetan's spiritual and political leader, writes in his book, *Voices from the Heart*, "I try to treat whomever I meet as an old friend. This gives me a genuine feeling of happiness. It is the practice of compassion."

Because we all share an identical need for love, it is possible to feel that anybody we meet, in whatever circumstances, is a brother or sister. So what are the attributes of those close, close, close friendships? Can you see these attributes as part of your psyche and a part of the connection with everyone you meet? Can every encounter have that kind of quality? Do you understand that each and every human being is no different than your truest friends? This would be a valuable quality to develop.

Charles M. Schwab, who leads the Bethlehem Steel Corporation, is the second largest steel maker in the United States and one of the most important manufacturers in the world. Schwab's advice is this: "Lead the life that will make you kindly and friendly to everyone about you, and you will be surprised what a happy life you will live."

SEEING THE SOUL

Whenever I fill out a form that asks me to check a box for my ethnicity, I mark "other" and write down "human." The point I am making is that I don't see race. I see souls. I mean it. When I meet people, I look at their soul, not their shape, gender, or color. I have a chapter in my book, *Secrets of the Bulletproof Spirit* titled, "When You See With Real Eyes, You Realize With Real Eyes." This came out of my meeting with Tony when I didn't see a murderer in him. Instead I saw another soul just like me.

I remember meeting a man named Gene. When a friend asked me what kind of a guy he was, I said, "He's a great guy."

"Well, is he black or white?" the friend asked.

"I don't remember. I didn't notice his skin color," I said quite honestly.

The truth is that purple is my favorite color so I always see people as purple. To me everybody's soul is purple. But if green is your favorite color, you could say that everybody's soul is green. You see, there are great lessons learned in deep friendships. If you have felt the joy of deep friendships, how can you bring this level of friendship to everyone you meet? If you haven't had any, you may be making judgments that are impeding your ability to develop quality friendships. It is important to remove any judgments and to connect on a soul level, looking through the eyes of empathy and compassion.

Sri Chinmoy, Indian spiritual teacher and philosopher, said, "Friendship openly persuades our minds to do the right thing and secretly convinces our hearts to become the right person."

FRIENDSHIPS MUST BE NOURISHED

I recently ended a relationship that I didn't have the time to nurture or develop. We did not invest the time to nurture and create a sustainable relationship. Looking back, it's obvious why this relationship didn't develop. Deep connections require being present for the other person, having no judgment, and allowing and accepting the other to be fully who they are without needing anything from them. Neither of us had made this kind of commitment.

The issue of judging oneself and others is something I have worked very hard on. We all have a lot of judgments – he's black, he's Christian, he's Muslim, he's fat, he's white, he's bald, he's greedy. One of TKF's key messages is "Everyone deserves to be loved and treated well."

Thomas Jefferson, our third US President and author of the Declaration of Independence, said, "Peace and friendship with all mankind is our wisest policy, and I wish we may be permitted to pursue it."

I am constantly bothered by race-oriented labels: Hispanic, but not white. Or Native American but not white. During the apartheid movement in South Africa, the Chinese were not considered white but the Japanese were, because they were pouring so much money into South Africa. We all live such busy lives today, myself included, so I really want to stress the importance of making it a priority to spend quality time with friends. If we get so busy that our friendships do not take precedence, we will be missing out on one of life's greatest joys. As Khalil Gibran writes, "Let there be no purpose in friendship save the deepening of the spirit."

CREATING LOVE AND UNITY FROM CONFLICT

From the time we are in grade school, we learn about and celebrate the great achievements and legacy of Martin Luther King Jr., a clergyman, activist, and prominent leader in the African-American civil rights movement. He stated, "Love is the only force capable of transforming an enemy into friend."

One of TKF's key messages is "From conflict you can create love and unity."

This was inspired by my relationship with Ples, which is a powerful example of friendship. He is a very important part of my life, and I'm a very important part of his life – and Tony's life, too. We have an incredibly deep bond – one that could have been tainted with anger and revenge, but instead it is a bond of love. Bahá'u'lláh, founder of the Bahá'í Faith said, "So powerful is the light of unity that it can illuminate the whole earth."

Ples and I have a genuine love for each other. It's not something we have to work at. We just feel it at a very deep level. I love being in his presence and giving him a hug. I feel tremendous love and support from him, too, and I often say that we are water bearers for each other.

Even though Tony took my son's life, and Ples was Tony's guardian and grandfather, we were still able to create a deep friendship. What was it in me that allowed us to get there? What was it in Ples?

PLES FELIX – MY BROTHER AND FRIEND

Ples offers his wise words on the subject of friendship:

"Friendship is an amazing dynamic when it is created. For me, friendship is both a privilege and a responsibility.

"The forgiveness with which Azim approached the murder of his son, was more than magnanimous. It was something that screamed out all this compassion and all this empathy. It really resonated deeply within me relative to my own compassion and empathy for Tariq's loss – his murder at the hands of my grandson. I immediately began to develop this sense of growing responsibility as a function of my own sense of understanding about death, dying, loss, grieving, and being in situations where the most sacred thing that we have, the thing that is as precious as our lives, is lost in an instant.

"There are no real words that we can say as human beings to properly honor and address that loss – or to even properly grieve it. Azim's initial response amplified my own sense of responsibility. So by the time that we actually met – as men, as human beings, as fathers – I had been doing so much praying and meditating – asking for guidance, seeking strength, desiring clarity and focus about how I could appropriately honor and try to address the loss of this precious person that was taken from the planet in a cruel act of senseless murder by my 14-year-old grandson.

"It was all I could do, with respect to my own sensibilities and my own spiritual practice, to seek guidance and to ask for an opportunity to look into the eyes of Tariq's parents, principally his father, because Azim was the person out front mostly and was the one I was most aware of. So I really focused on meeting with him – wanting to share my deep grief for the loss of his son, and to extend to him my deepest sympathy and to also express verbally my commitment to be of support to him and his family in any way that I could.

"In that initial meeting, both Azim and I being able to look into each other's eyes and see each other as God-spirited people – God-spirited men – not seeking retribution, not hiding in anger in any way, but both having the tremendous burden of a loss – he the loss of his son – me the loss of my grandson to the penitentiary system. Being in that space in that initial meeting, we both did not want anything more than to be of support to each other and beyond that to be of support to other kids and other families far beyond our own.

"Our friendship developed and continues to grow based on my own sense of responsibility and the privilege that continues to develop in stride with the nature and the quality and the richness of the camaraderie – the mutual human support that Azim and I are to each other personally and by our example, our friendship and our continued support of each other, to the Tariq Khamisa Foundation and to other children and all the wonderful people who have come together in the spirit of TKF.

"That really fortifies and validates the privilege of the friendship and the promise that our brotherhood and our love for each other will continue to serve as an example to others who may not have lost as much or may have lost much more. The friendship that Azim and I have as brothers and friends and fathers and grandfathers is something that enriches me; it enlivens me; it inspires me, and it really fuels me because it feeds both the responsibilities and the privileges of friendship – all born from a place of tragedy that is undergoing constant and continual healing in the presence of compassion, empathy and forgiveness."

FRIENDS REFLECT OUR PERCEPTION

I love a particular story in Dr. Wayne Dyer's book *Real Magic*. Dr. Dyer is walking on the beach in Hawaii and a man comes up to him and asks, "Do you live here?"

"Yes," Dr. Dyer answers.

The man asks, "What are the people in Hawaii like?"

"Well, where are you from?" Dr. Dyer asks him.

The man says, "I'm from New York."

"What are the people like in New York?" Dr. Dyer asks.

"Oh," the man responds, "they're rude, they don't have any time for you, and they're not friendly."

Dr. Dyer says," Well, you'll find people like that here too – similar to the people in New York."

Then he walks down the beach further and he meets a man from Atlanta.

"What are people in Atlanta like?" Dr. Dyer asks.

The man responds, "They're very friendly, they're hospitable, they're kind, they're generous."

"In Hawaii, most of the people are just like that too," Dr. Dyer answers.

I guess you can see the point here.

One of my all time favorite quotes is by Rumi, a 13th-century Persian poet, Islamic jurist, theologian, and mystic. I believe the field he speaks about below is the field of love and friendship: "Out beyond ideas of wrongdoing and right doing, there is a field. I will meet you there."

CHAPTER SIX

TRUST

Sustained trust creates empathy.

~ Azim Khamisa, The Peace Formula

The basis of any relationship is trust. And along with trust is respect. I don't think you can ever respect anyone whom you don't trust. But trust has to be won and it takes a long time – especially today because of the kind of society we live in.

The founder of Buddhism Gautama Buddha said, "Health is the greatest gift, contentment the greatest wealth, faithfulness the best relationship."

I grew up in a small town in Kenya. Everybody knew everybody, and we didn't have a lot of lawyers and lawsuits like we do in our society today. In the Kenyan business world, one's reputation got around very quickly and the community knew the trustworthy. We knew who had a high level of integrity, morals and values. There was never any worry about whether they were people of high integrity. We all just knew. I remember doing business with people on a handshake. And a lot of money exchanged hands on those handshakes! You knew that person had the kind of reputation that could never be compromised. Indira Gandhi, India's first and, to date, only female Prime Minister, said, "You can't shake hands with a clenched fist."

When I lived in Kenya, which was a neighboring country to Uganda where dictator Idi Amin forced out many of my family members, we all felt threatened. While we left Kenya voluntarily, we lost a lot of material possessions and the Kenyan currency was not legally transferable.

We had to get money out essentially on the black market, which meant we had to trust people because we had to give them our cash. I remember working with someone who was an exporter. I would give him cash, and when I went to London, he would give me back the equivalent in pounds. There was no transaction record and he could've said, "What cash?" But amazingly, I never lost a dime.

There were also times when I helped people get their money out after I had learned how to do it. When someone gave me their cash, they trusted me to give it back to them, and I always did, happy to help them make a new start like I had to. You had to be trustworthy to function in that environment, and your reputation and your business was based on that trust, which in turn led to respect. People would come to you because you were known as a trustworthy upstanding citizen, worthy of respect.

LACK OF TRUST IN OUR SOCIETY TODAY

Gautama Buddha said, "There is nothing more dreadful than the habit of doubt. Doubt separates people. It is a poison that disintegrates friendships and breaks up pleasant relations. It is a thorn that irritates and hurts; it is a sword that kills."

If you look at our world today, there are more than 200,000 lawyers in California alone. Compare this to 20,000 lawyers in the entire country of Japan with a population of 128 million people. To me, this demonstrates that the most popular sport in California is not football, baseball, or basketball, but rather, lawsuits – all because there is so little trust.

It is typical in this society for people to enter into business deals much too quickly and to sign documents right away.

I had a client whose modus operandi was basically to get into partnership with other clients and then sue them because he was a lawyer. But what kind of tactic is that? Lawsuits have become a game and business has become a strategy that is totally immoral. Just look at the chaos on Wall Street, due to greed and people taking advantage of each other – all in the pursuit of the almighty dollar.

Many of these situations end up in extremely expensive lawsuits. This does not happen everywhere, though. In smaller, less financially oriented societies, businesses operate on a handshake – a commitment to doing what they say they are going to do.

Over the years, I have stopped attracting clients whom I don't trust or respect (people who would go behind my back or accept bribes) like I did earlier in my business. Today, I have honed my skills to feel energetically who someone is and what they want. When I meet someone whom I feel is not in his or her integrity, I tell them that I'm too busy to help them right now. I have certainly been in situations where I might have chosen to sue, but I didn't. I felt it was easier to attract new clients than risking getting a reputation as someone who likes to sue. I simply use my mistakes as lessons and do my best never to repeat them.

BEING RESPECTABLE

It is essential, both in business and in personal relationships, that trust and respect are not missing. Ralph Waldo Emerson, American Poet and Essayist said, "Men are respectable only as they respect."

A big part of getting there is to maintain a very high standard for yourself, so that others see you as a respected individual. When you are clear and transparent with no secret agendas, it will be obvious to others that you are speaking the truth. You are creating a reputation where people can say without a doubt, "Yes, I can trust this person." A relationship without respect will be unfulfilling and will not bring you peace.

The truth is that trust and respect are hard to create and are very easily lost. To be at peace, you need to live from a place of trust and respect. Since I like to give people the benefit of the doubt, I start my evaluation of someone else with an open mind and an expectation of their trustworthiness. Then, if they show me that I can't trust them, I let them go. When you're aligned – when your truth is the whole truth – you will be able to see yourself and your relationships through compassionate confrontation and forgiveness.

WHAT DOES LOVE LOOK LIKE?

Why is love so important?

French writer George Sand said, There is only one way of happiness, in life: to love and be loved.

Buddha said, "Hatred does not cease by hatred, but only by love; this is the eternal rule."

German writer, Johann Goethe said, "Only the soul that loves is happy."

Without love and happiness, both high vibratory emotions emanating from the soul, it is impossible to have peace. Trust and respect are essential elements for empathy, love and happiness to blossom. The Dalai Lama, Tibetan spiritual and political leader, says, "Because we all share an identical need for love, it is possible to feel that anybody we meet, in whatever circumstances, is a brother or sister."

Saint Augustine says: "It has the hands to help others. It has the feet to hasten to the poor and needy. It has eyes to see misery and want. It has the ears to hear the sighs and sorrows of men. That is what love looks like. Since love grows within you, so beauty grows. For love is the beauty of the soul."

We must also remind ourselves of the profound words of St. Francis of Assisi: "Lord, grant that I might not so much seek to be loved as to love."

I have often wondered why so many spiritual masters like the Dalai Lama, Thich Naht Hanh and various orders of monks have all taken the oath of celibacy. I never really understood this although I have the highest regard for these luminaries. Gandhi became celibate at the age of 36. But why?

Thich Naht Hanh, is an expatriate Vietnamese Zen Buddhist monk, teacher, author, poet and peace activist. In an article titled, *"The Third Precept: Sexual Responsibility,"* he states:

Monks and nuns do not engage in sexual relationships because they want to devote their energy to having a breakthrough in meditation. They learn to channel their sexual energy to strengthen their spirit energy for the breakthrough. They also practice deep breathing to increase the spirit energy. Since they live alone, without a family, they can devote most of their time to meditation and teaching, helping the people who provide them with food, shelter, and so on.

I believe that the majority of people reading this book are not interested in becoming celibate monks. Most of us want a significant relationship because through healthy, loving, deep, intimate relationships, we are rewarded with balance and spiritual growth. Do you have a relationship that provides this?

My friends, Donna and Glenn Pinto, have been happily married since 1995. They are like yin and yang, and I wanted to know their secret. I wanted to know the essential elements for a happy and fulfilling relationship that lasts.

Donna told me that one of her favorite quotes is: "Love is not gazing into each other's eyes; it is looking together in the same direction."

She went on to say, "My relationship with Glenn grew out of a two-year friendship. Love blossomed slowly over time. I remember early in our relationship, visiting Glenn's home in NY and watching him interact with his mom and sister. I knew this was a special man who was dedicated and loving towards his family. That was something that meant a lot to me coming from parents who divorced when I was 14 and left me wondering if I could ever trust a man to not hurt me like my dad hurt my mom, me and my siblings. With Glenn I felt safe, comforted and totally free to be myself.

"We did not have a traditional courtship of dating. We met while working at Club Med in Mexico and were friends while working together for two years. We both had a desire to travel around the world – to not follow the conventional career path – and to encourage others to do the same. Conversations about writing a book to inspire other young people to take time out to live, work or volunteer abroad turned into reality. Within a year, we were planning a "research trip" that ended up doubling as a honeymoon around the world. We knew we were soul mates – we just felt we were meant to be together to live out our passions.

"Traveling to 20 countries and being together every day was wonderful. We simply enjoyed each other's company and even made a great team running a ski chalet in Norway for five months of our two-year sojourn. Our relationship is grounded in a rich history and foundation of supporting one another to be ourselves and live out our passions.

"We still encourage one another to do everything we want, and because we allow each other this freedom, we are able to blossom individually and bring joy not only to our relationship, but also to our two children, our friends, our extended family and to those we interact with through work and life. We have tremendous respect for each other and total trust. From the first time I watched Glenn interact with his family, I knew he would be a great husband and dad. Years later, I am still counting my blessings daily and I feel this from Glenn as well. It is with this deep appreciation, respect and trust for each other that our love continues to blossom."

INSIGHTS ON LOVE & LASTING RELATIONSHIPS

Thich Naht Hanh offers some beautiful insights into what makes relationships last. He writes:

> There are two Vietnamese words, "tinh" and "nghia," that are difficult to translate into English. They both mean something like love. In tinh, you

find elements of passion. It can be very deep, absorbing the whole of your being. Nghia is a kind of continuation of tinh. With nghia you feel much calmer, more understanding, more willing to sacrifice to make the other person happy, and more faithful. You are not as passionate as in tinh, but your love is deeper and more solid. Nghia will keep you and the other person together for a long time. It is the result of living together and sharing difficulties and joy over time.

In nghia, you feel gratitude for the other person. Thank you for having chosen me. Thank you for being my husband or my wife. There are so many people in society, why have you chosen me? I am very thankful. That is the beginning of nghia, the sense of thankfulness for your having chosen me as your companion to share the best things in yourself, as well as your suffering and your happiness.

Children, if they observe deeply, will see that what keeps their parents together is nghia and not passionate love. If their parents take good care of each other, look after each other with calmness, tenderness, and care, nghia is the foundation of that care. That is the kind of love we really need for our family and for our society.

Rabindranath Tagore, one of my favorite poets, describes love this way: "To understand anything is to find in it something which is our own, and it is the discovery of ourselves outside us which makes us glad. This relation of understanding is partial, but the relation of love is complete. In love the sense of difference is obliterated and the human soul fulfills its purpose in perfection, transcending the limits of itself and reaching across the threshold of the infinite. Therefore love is the highest bliss that man can attain to, for through it alone he truly knows that he is more than himself, and that he is at one with the All."

A LETTER FROM DONNA

My dear friend, Donna, wrote the following essay about her life's transformation after she heard one of my speeches. I am including it here, not because it speaks of me. But rather, I am including it because she articulates her transformation so well. I was particularly moved by her expression of "being the change," and "inviting the divine into her life."

Being the Change I Wish to See in the World

At age 15, my best friend Lynette died after we shared a helicopter "life flight" to Westlake Hospital in Los Angeles. Separated only by a curtain in the emergency room, I couldn't see her, but I knew before the nurse told me that she didn't make it. From that point on, I have been on what some might call a spiritual quest – looking for clues to the meaning of life. "When the student is ready, the teacher appears" is a phrase I have used often. Yet now, I was not only ready, I was eager and asking to be shown how to turn years of self-inquiry and insights gleaned from books and seminars into action.

My answer came to me through my headphones while listening to a conference on tape called "Awakening A Global Vision." A soft-spoken man with a beautiful accent, Azim Khamisa, told his extremely personal and heart-wrenching story in a speech called "Collective Wisdom and Spiritual Activism."

In 1995, Mr. Khamisa's 20-year-old son, Tariq, was murdered while delivering pizzas. The bullet that tore through Tariq's body was shot by Tony Hicks, a 14-year-old boy who was handed a gun by an 18-year-old gang member and given the order "bust him bone."

The one and only shot fired was fatal. Tony Hicks became the first juvenile to be tried as an adult in the state of California. He was sentenced to 25 years to life in prison. This tragic incident, resulting from a series of poor choices, sent one youth to the grave and one to prison, and changed the lives of their loved ones forever.

But the amazing part of the story is that Azim, the father of Tariq, did not respond with anger and rage towards Tony, his son's assailant. Through endless hours of deep meditation, Azim had a profound realization. In his words, he said "I saw victims at both ends of the gun." The rage he felt was not directed at Tony, but at a society that placed a young boy too young to drive on a dark street holding a handgun. After founding the Tariq Khamisa Foundation, astonishingly, Azim decided to reach out in forgiveness to Ples Felix, the grandfather and guardian of Tony. Ples gladly accepted the invitation to help Azim in creating an organization with the mission of saving other children and families from being affected by the epidemic of youth violence in our culture.

Losing his only son was Azim Khamisa's defining moment – the BIG AHA that would transform his pleasant life as an international investment banker into what he calls a "spiritual activist" and a social worker, which he claims was a step up in his career.

After listening to this story, I had what I call a revelation. I literally wept like a baby in the shower at my gym. Picturing the sight of Azim standing in Tariq's grave, as he described, being handed the body of his dead son, a ritual of his Islamic faith, I was practically hyperventilating. I couldn't help but think of my children, Skyler, age 6 and Cody, age 4... I simply could not imagine.

For me, this story touched a nerve. I was reminded of my own personal tragedies and the unspeakable pain of loss that Azim described. I thought of my brother, who, at the age of twelve, was accosted and victimized by a child predator. I thought of the fateful day my friend Lynette and I were thrown from the back of her cousin's pick-up truck while going 50 miles per hour – flinging us like rag dolls through the air onto the hard black pavement. These were the defining moments in my life – the pivotal points that put me directly onto a deeper, more meaningful, spiritual path.

Yet now, 26 years after my own near death experience and the loss of my friend, I stood in the shower sobbing. A flood of feelings and tears poured out of me. Listening to Azim Khamisa describe how he transformed his despair into forgiveness, healing and spiritual activism ignited something in me. In that moment I was able to see that everything that had happened in my life – the good and the bad, the tragedy and the triumph, had all brought me to this moment. Suddenly an ocean of gratitude washed over me. Loud and clear, it was as if my true calling in life was being revealed to me … as though for the first time I could see and hear the beautiful gift being given to me.

It is a gift available to all who allow themselves to feel deeply and to see that there truly is mystical meaning in everything. To then take action for something because you are compelled to do so – called to give of yourself and live for a higher and grander purpose. To not look away, but rather to look deeply and to feel deeply – this is where it is possible to find your life calling. I know. From my deepest despair, I found mine.

In an instant it became crystal clear to me. I knew that I had to step up and be a leader – an example for my children, for other children and for parents everywhere. I could no longer sit idly by on the sidelines. To quote

Mahatma Ghandi, I had to "be the change that I wished to see in the world." Although I felt proud and privileged to be a stay-at-home mom, I knew that there was something more that I needed to do. I, like Azim Khamisa, had to become a spiritual activist.

Eager to put my insights and feelings into action, within a few weeks I filled journals that had sat empty for years with new and exciting ideas and visions. I suddenly felt like some kind of powerful force was pushing me. I surrendered to it. I felt surges of creativity, energy, enthusiasm and passion. Ideas flowed effortlessly.

I soon found myself e-mailing the director of my son's preschool an idea and a page of notes for an "International Peace Camp." This became the school's six-week summer camp theme called "Passport to Peace." One little seed planted for a happier, more peaceful world, I thought.

Almost immediately after hearing Azim's story, I started volunteering the very little childfree time I had with the Tariq Khamisa Foundation. Witnessing one of their 4th – 6th grade school assemblies was life-changing for me as well as the children. I thought everyone needs to hear this story.

As I became more aware of my life purpose, I suddenly felt drawn to things that I hadn't noticed before. For months I had walked straight by a banner "Support Americans for a Department of Peace (AFDOP)" at the Unity Church my family occasionally attended. Now I felt magnetized to it and I made the time to attend a meeting. This is where I found my "tribe." These are ordinary people with humungous hearts – souls who give freely of their time and energy for a beautiful goal – the establishment of a cabinet level U.S. Department of Peace which would support organizations like TKF and others who are already teaching and implementing youth violence prevention and nonviolent solutions to domestic and international conflict.

It was through AFDOP that I met Jill, a mom with young kids like me, who recently founded Kids for Peace – a delightful group of kids ages 3 -11. My children Skyler and Cody have enjoyed monthly meetings where they have painted peace flags, sung songs and made "peace packs" filled with toiletries and other goodies for children in remote villages of Nepal, Thailand and Nicaragua. Family and friends eagerly sponsored Cody and Skyler in their first fundraiser – a Walk for Peace. Checks with happy faces magically appeared in our mailbox! Skyler and Cody were thrilled to have raised $350 to contribute to more Kids for Peace projects!

In a matter of a few months my life as a stay-at-home mom has been enriched in ways I couldn't have imagined. I am now simply watching events serendipitously unfold, "peace angels" appear and inspiration arise. I am teaching my children about getting involved. Together we are participating in service projects, social action, peace building and fundraising – all for the betterment of our community and our world. I am proud to say with conviction that I am now leading by example and being the change I wish to see in the world.

Donna's story of "being the change" is a good example of "inviting the divine" into her life. It was from a state of surrender that she was "asking to be shown how to turn years of self-inquiry and insights gleaned from books and seminars into action." The answer was given. It was the asking that brought forth her life calling. In Matthew 7:7, Jesus states, "Ask, and it will be given to you; seek, and you will find; knock, and it will be opened to you."

"Come out of the circle of time, and into the circle of love."

~ Rumi, 13th century theologian and mystic

CHAPTER SEVEN

EMPATHY

Sustained empathy creates compassion.

~ Azim Khamisa, The Peace Formula

Kids today choose to join gangs for many reasons. Tony did that, too, at the age of eleven. If I had joined a gang when I was eleven and had the same kind of life that Tony had, who knows if I might have done what he did. Gandhi said, "Hate the sin; love the sinner." Empathy helps us look at an offense in a different way.

Empathy can be defined as: "Identification with and understanding of another's situation, feelings, and motives."

When I began to truly turn to my empathy, when I took the time to understand where Tony had come from and why he was on his particular journey, I knew exactly why he did what he did. Here was an 11-year-old who had just joined a gang, who was already addicted to drugs and alcohol, and at age fourteen, had killed an innocent person to prove himself to the gang.

So who is the culprit here? If you say it's Tony, that doesn't speak to our present society. But if you say the culprit is the societal pressure that forced an African American boy to join a gang at eleven and take the life of an innocent human being when he was fourteen to prove himself to the gang, then we can use that information to improve our society.

These kinds of horrific killings take place much too often in our culture, and not only among African American males.

Although the majority is African American, many youngsters who join gangs are Caucasian, Hispanic, and Asian. According to the Sourcebook of Criminal Justice Statistics, the likelihood of incarceration for African Americans (16.2 percent) is almost twice that of Hispanics (9.4 percent) and more than six times that of Caucasians (2.5 percent). Among men, African Americans have a 28.5 percent chance of incarceration over their lifetime, while Hispanics have a 16.2 percent chance and Caucasians have a 4.4 percent chance. Approximately 10-11 percent of Americans are African American and approximately 70 percent are in jail.

TRANSFORM EMPATHY INTO LOVE AND COMPASSION

In his book, *Teachings on Love,* Thich Nhat Hanh writes, "Continue until you see yourself in the cruelest person on earth, in the child starving, in the political prisoner. Practice until you recognize yourself in everyone in the supermarket, on the street corner, in a concentration camp, on a leaf, in a dewdrop. Meditate until you see yourself in a speck of dust in a distant galaxy. See and listen with the whole of your being. If you are fully present, the rain of Dharma will water the deepest seeds in your store consciousness, and tomorrow, while you are washing the dishes or looking at the blue sky, that seed will spring forth, and love and understanding will appear as a beautiful flower."

Because I had empathy for Tony, I was able to start working to prevent more young people from becoming like he was when he killed my son. I was able to take my distressed energy and put it into something useful for society and at the same time, it brought a lot more meaning in my own life.

TKF has been teaching empathy to kids who would otherwise never come to know and feel it in this world. Our organization describes empathy as the ability to relate to how another person feels, and we have lessons on the topics of both respect and empathy. At the beginning of the lesson, students watch a powerful TKF video titled "Everyone Deserves to Be Loved and Treated Well." This is one of a six-part video series called "Ending The Cycle of Violence."

After students watch the video, they review the TKF story and are asked the following questions:

- Think about the last time you felt respected by someone. What did they do?

- Think about a time when you showed empathy for someone. Describe the circumstances. How did it feel?

- How do you think Azim was able to show empathy for Tony?

WHO'S BEEN IN MY SHOES?

We do an activity at TKF that helps students understand and cultivate empathy. A key aspect about empathy is that you can't really have it for somebody you don't know. This is why we take kids through the exercise "Who's been in my shoes."

The students take hands and form a circle. Then the leader says, "In order to practice empathy toward someone else, it helps to try and put yourself in their shoes. In other words, it helps to see the world from another's perspective."

First we emphasize that you don't know someone until you have walked a mile in his or her shoes. Then a volunteer stands in the center of the circle and starts a sentence with: "You've been in my shoes if you have ever..." Students add a personal quality, experience or something else that they may have in common with others. Some examples could be:

- You've been in my shoes - if you've ever had to take care of your little sister.

- You've been in my shoes - if you've ever laughed so hard that juice came out of your nose.

- You've been in my shoes - if you've ever had to serve detention.

- You've been in my shoes - if you've ever sung a song really loud when no one else was around.

Any student who has had the same experience crosses the circle and takes a seat in an empty chair. Since there is one less chair than people, whoever has nowhere to sit goes into the center of the circle and becomes the speaker.

When the activity is over, the leader asks the students what they learned. Do they see that they have more in common with their classmates than they thought? These kinds of bonds help to foster equanimity and empathy among our kids at TKF, who are without a doubt among the most vulnerable and at-risk youths.

YOU DON'T KNOW ME UNTIL...

You cannot have empathy for someone you don't know. Alex, a middle school Hispanic student who went through TKF's lesson on empathy, is a good example.

One day Alex was walking in his "hood" when another kid, an African American, gave him an angry look. In the hood, if someone from another hood gives you an angry look, that's reason enough to beat them up. But after going through TKF's lesson on empathy, Alex realized he didn't know why this kid was giving him an angry look. Instead of throwing a punch, he asked the kid, "Why did you give me a dirty look?" The boy responded, "I didn't give you a dirty look. I'm angry because my brother was shot and killed."

What did Alex do? He reached out to him and said, "I know how you feel because my uncle was killed six months ago."

Because Alex had learned about empathy, what might have been a violent incident became a compassionate meeting of the minds. Someone who previously resorted to violence was now communicating compassionately. When Alex walks in the hoods now, he walks with empathy and compassion.

If we use Alex as a role model, we can see that we don't have much empathy for people we don't know. Muslims are a good example right now because the media focuses on those Muslims who inflict harm. But this is not the norm. When you get to know most Muslims, you will find that they are not much different from you.

You can call yourself empathic when someone does something with which you don't agree, but you don't judge them. Instead you ask yourself, "How would I have functioned in the same situation? How would I feel if I was forced to do something because my life depended on it?"

With empathy, we can see that we are all fallible, that we are all human, that we all have the same needs, that we all want to stop suffering, and that we all want happiness. We are not separate, then, but we are one. Whenever we meet someone, however different from us they may seem, we need to understand that they have the same needs as we do.

In our forgiveness workshops, we do an exercise called "Just Like Me." This helps to develop empathy with someone who is hard to connect with. The exercise below will only take a few minutes and will help you understand someone else so much better.

On a piece of paper, write the name of someone you want to forgive and what you are forgiving them for. Now, keep your mind focused on that person and repeat the statements below:

Just like me, (their name) is seeking happiness in his/her life.

Just like me, (their name) is trying to avoid suffering in his/her life.

Just like me, (their name) has engaged in behavior that was motivated by fear.

Just like me, (their name) has known sorrow, loss, loneliness, hopelessness

Just like me, (their name) is seeking fulfillment in his/her life.

Just like me, (their name) is learning about life.

Just like me, (their name), if offered an opportunity, would make a different decision.

Just like me, (their name) is not perfect.

Just like me, (their name) is . . . write a statement that applies to your situation.

This is a valuable exercise for those of us who are in the habit of rejecting and blaming people who appear to be different. We don't know the Iraqis or the Iranian and they really don't know each other. The Palestinians and Israelis don't know one another, which makes it easy to demonize each other. But if you are a world traveler, "just like me," and you get to know people in foreign lands, you'll see that everyone wants the same things – to stop suffering and just be happy.

JUDGMENT: THE OPPOSITE OF EMPATHY

When you first meet someone, do you focus on how they are different from you, or do you place your attention on how they are the same as you? We often look at other people with an outward smile, while inwardly we are thinking, "What a funny looking outfit she's wearing." Or "He's really getting bald. He looked so much better when he had a full head of hair."

This is judgment, the opposite of empathy, and we engage in it every time we criticize someone. What do you think when you meet someone with a big bolt screwed into their lips or ears? Do you judge, or are you interested in finding out more about that person who is clearly very different from you. The same thing happens in politics. That which is politically correct here may be the opposite in another part of the world.

A passage in the Bible reminds us about judging. From Luke 6:35-38;42:

"But love your enemies, do good to them, and lend to them without expecting to get anything back. Then your reward will be great, and you will be sons of the Most High, because he is kind to the ungrateful and wicked. Be merciful, just as your Father is merciful. "Do not judge, and you will not be judged. Do not condemn, and you will not be condemned. Forgive, and you will be forgiven. Give, and it will be given to you. A good measure, pressed down, shaken together and running over, will be poured into your lap. For with the measure you use, it will be measured to you." ... How can you say to your brother, 'Brother, let me take the speck out of your eye,' when you yourself fail to see the plank in your own eye? You hypocrite, first take the plank out of your eye, and then you will see clearly to remove the speck from your brother's eye."

If you have a highly developed sense of empathy, when you come across someone who may appear different or foreign, then you are able to think: "Their needs are no different than mine. This is another soul who is on the same journey. They may be simply at a different spot along the journey. How can I have this encounter and deepen my sense of empathy and maybe promote a deeper sense of empathy in them?"

By cultivating a deep sense of empathy, we put ourselves in a better frame of mind, which will wipe out judgment. Remember that judgment is separation, while empathy is unity.

EMPATHY: THE PRECURSER FOR COMPASSION

To quote Thich Naht Hanh once again, "You can't forgive until compassion is born in your heart." But you can't have compassion until you have empathy.

Saint Augustine said, "Seek not to understand that you may believe, but believe that you may understand."

In order to cultivate empathy it is important to look at the relationships in your life with your family, friends and coworkers. Are you happy with these relationships? If you are not, I think that's a sign that you need to deepen your sense of empathy. It's time to consider other people's needs instead of thinking about only your own. This is a hard one because our tendency is to do the exact opposite. And so, this takes practice. It is only in doing it over and over that you can make this forward step. I have become a big doer, not just a thinker or a reader. Whatever I intend to teach, I am adamant about putting it into action for myself first.

Cultivating empathy has helped me succeed as a consultant in investment banking and in my nonprofit work. I always make sure to go the extra mile, and we impress this upon our kids at TFK. We emphasize to them that the choices they make affect not only them. Those choices have a huge impact on others as well, including their loved ones as well as a plethora of people they don't know. I use the example of Tony – how his choices and actions impacted his mom, his grandfather, his teachers, his classmates, Tariq, Tariq's fiancé Jennifer and her family, Tariq's sister, Tasreen, his mom, Almas, myself, and many others who are connected to each of us.

The problem was of course, that when Tony pulled the trigger, he wasn't thinking of anybody, including himself.

Gautama Buddha said, "He who experiences the unity of life sees his own Self in all beings, and all beings in his own Self, and looks on everything with an impartial eye."

Psychologist Carl Jung said, "Your vision will become clear only when you look into your heart … Who looks outside, dreams. Who looks inside, awakens."

When we look within and meditate on our own heart, we will know that we are not separate – we are one. We share one heart, one soul, and are one with all life. What we do to another, we do to ourselves. When we are in empathy, we are as Rabrindranath Tagore says, "one with the all…"

CHAPTER EIGHT

COMPASSION

Sustained compassion creates peace.

~ Azim Khamisa, The Peace Formula

Thich Naht Hanh says, "Unless compassion is born in your heart, you cannot forgive." This means that compassion is the precursor to forgiveness. I see compassion as the ability to feel the humanity in all human beings. When I met Tony five years after the tragedy, I asked Ples to give Tony and me some time alone. Tony was the last person to see Tariq alive, and I wanted him to fill in some of the blanks for me about Tariq's last moments.

Tony and I spent about two and a half hours together that day. I remember it was somewhere in the middle of our visit when I just looked into his eyes for a long time. I was trying to see the "murderer" in him, but I didn't see it. I felt that as I climbed through his eyes, instead of seeing a murderer, I was able to feel his soul and touch his humanity.

Sure, he did something very wrong. He took the life of my son – an innocent, unarmed person. The worst thing you can do is to take the life of a human being. But, that did not make Tony inhuman. This, I think, is where compassion is very important.

If we truly are compassionate, then we remain compassionate in all circumstances. Even though there may be dark aspects of a person, we have to remember that we are one. We are all connected at a soul level, and each of us is on a different level of our soul's journey. Whoever crosses our path does so for a reason, and it is often the worst of situations – like mine – that brings us to our soul's purpose.

COMPASSION: THE HIGHEST VIBRATION

Even when someone does something very wrong, like Tony did, it behooves us to refrain from judgment. Judgment exists in a very low energetic vibratory frequency. On the other hand, compassion exists in a very high vibratory frequency. Therefore, it is important to live in compassion and remain in the space of high vibration.

I don't see a lot of compassion in business meetings or in personal interactions. What I usually see is a lot of ego. I see people who are so into themselves, they are busy positioning to win as if life were a football field! Have you noticed how often people interrupt you when you're speaking about something? They aren't listening since they are already thinking of what they want to say. This is the ego coming out and it clearly shows a lack of compassion. When we are controlled by ego, it is impossible to be compassionate. But when you are in compassion, you are not trying to one-up someone else or beat them at the pass.

A compassionate person sits back and listens. He or she doesn't judge and is able to see the humanity in the other person. Compassionate people are not self-occupied. If you are always thinking about ME, ME, ME, ME, ME – that's not compassion. It's self-indulgence. I used to be that way when Tariq was alive, so I should know. I was very much about ME, ME, ME, ME, ME. But Tariq's death built compassion in me. Today, everything is not so much about ME anymore. I am no longer preoccupied with myself alone. When I meet somebody, I'm no longer interested in trying to one-up someone or get the last word. It's not about that for me. Now it's about compassion. It's about sitting back and feeling the humanity of the other person.

As we discussed in the chapter on empathy, the exercise "Just Like Me" helps people understand that we are all human beings and we all want the same things. The Dalai Lama often says everybody wants to be happy and nobody wants to suffer. I agree and so I focus on having compassion and helping other people end their suffering, because that will end my suffering, too.

THE "PASSION" IN COMPASSION

Compassion contains the word "passion." Compassionate people have passion for what they are doing. In my case, if I hadn't worked to build my compassion, I wouldn't be good at what I do. It is ironic that my work, which resulted from the tragedy of losing Tariq, is far more fulfilling and has more meaning than my work as an investment banker ever had. It is nurturing to me because I believe I am making a difference, and I feel a high vibratory emotion when I am engaged in what I do working at many levels of society teaching others how to achieve peace, prosperity and purpose through the practice of forgiveness. And I believe that the passion I have for this work makes me a more compassionate human being.

Mitch Albom, author of *Tuesdays With Morrie*, said, "The way you get meaning into your life is to devote yourself to loving others, devote yourself to your community around you, and devote yourself to creating something that gives you purpose and meaning."

If you have no passion for what you're doing, you will have a hard time developing compassion. Whatever your lifestyle, whatever your work, it is important to love what you do. Some of us have many roles, and if passion is missing in any one of them, there is most likely something you need to let go of.

I understand that being compassionate all the time, like the Dalai Lama or Thich Nhat Hanh have achieved, is not easy for us regular folk. I have worked hard on it, and maybe I have more compassion than I used to, but I still have a long way to go before I can be there all the time, or even most of the time. But I am making progress.

When I think about Tony, my blood pressure doesn't go up any more. Actually, these days, thinking about Tony makes me feel calm. His presence has a safe passage through my mind now – a true sign that I have forgiven him. But it has taken a great deal of time and effort. If there are issues in your life such as estranged relationships or resentments and guilt, you will have a hard time being compassionate about anything until those issues are resolved. For that reason alone, I have dedicated a great deal of time learning to forgive and helping others to do the same. Developing compassion is one of my greatest motivations for creating a variety of rich tools that teach forgiveness and compassion, step-by-step, through my website, books and workshops.

COMPASSION IS OUR TRUE NATURE

The Thich Naht Hanh quote that began this chapter, "Unless compassion is born in your heart, you cannot forgive," means that compassion is the precursor to forgiveness. But forgiveness is also a precursor to compassion. They go hand-in-hand. When we forgive and resolve our issues, we automatically have more empathy and we develop more compassion. This ultimately leads us to peace. Here are three essential points to remember:

1. Compassion is about feeling the humanity in everyone we meet.

2. Passion is part of compassion.

3. Forgive and resolve your issues to achieve compassion.

Do you recall a time when you felt compassionate? Do you remember how euphoric it was? Now remember when you felt judgmental. How did that feel? Not so euphoric. We simply cannot be judgmental and euphoric at the same time, just like we can't be happy and angry at the same time. But we can be happy if we are compassionate which is our natural state of being.

Thich Nhat Hanh describes it this way: "The essence of love and compassion is understanding, the ability to recognize the physical, material, and psychological suffering of others, to put ourselves 'inside the skin' of the other. We go inside their body, feelings, and mental formations, and witness for ourselves their suffering. Shallow observation as an outsider is not enough to see their suffering. We must become one with the subject of our observation. When we are in contact with another's suffering, a feeling of compassion is born in us. Compassion means, literally, to suffer with."

The Dalai Lama says that a tiger's true nature is to be aggressive. That's why it has claws and fangs. But he reminds us that human beings do not have claws and fangs. Rather, we have flat teeth for chewing and modest-looking nails. Hence, it is our true nature to be compassionate. But we must experience compassion at a deep level in our souls to truly recognize it. Then, once you can experience it during some special moments in your life – with your child, with your husband or wife, and with your friends – the question arises: How can you live in that space all the time?

The Dalai Lama talks about when the Chinese had killed about 1.6 million Tibetans, many of them monks. According to CNN US News, more than 6,000 Tibetan monasteries have been destroyed since China occupied Tibet in 1959 and many monks were taken as prisoners. One of them was a childhood friend of the Dalai Lama, and was in a Chinese prison for 30-plus years and was tortured severely.

But because he was a high-ranking monk, the Chinese eventually released him due to international pressure. He traveled from China to India to pay homage to the Dalai Lama, the secular and spiritual leader of the Tibetan people.

The Dalai Lama said that they hugged and sat down to tea together. When his friend said that in the Chinese prison, he had a feeling of "impending danger" in his life, the Dalai Lama asked, "Were you afraid the Chinese were going to kill you?"

"No," the Monk said, "I was not afraid of dying. The impending danger in my life was that I would lose compassion for the Chinese."

I cried when I heard this story because I experienced some of the basics of his teachings. If I had lost compassion for Tony and Ples, where would I be? What do you replace that with? When you finally get to a level where you realize that you're in compassion most of the time, your world looks very different. You're a magnet and you attract people. You have better relationships. You're not so preoccupied with yourself. You're more involved with the world. You feel a deep connection with humanity at large and with each individual human being in the world.

RITUAL AS A WAY OF LIFE

To build compassion, we must remember that we are all fallible and we all make mistakes. We are one human race, created in different tribes and nations so that we can learn to understand each other. All of the "isms" are man-made. According to the Koran, the prophet Muhammad taught us that all human beings were formed into nations and tribes "so that we may know one another, not to conquer, subjugate, revile or slaughter, but to reach out toward others with intelligence and understanding."

We've all heard the adage "variety is the spice of life." It would be a very strange world if we were all blonde and blue-eyed or brunette and brown-eyed. We can learn to appreciate the variety in religions, cultures, colors and race because diversity creates richness. It gives us the opportunity to understand why a culture does something in a certain way. These things fascinate me because there is always an interesting reason behind everything. We may judge others because we do things differently, but when we understand the reason others do what they do, we can appreciate that it makes sense.

Having a natural curiosity and desire to learn about different cultures is a great way to build compassion. In Africa where I grew up, the Maasai tribe is very ritualistic. I have always been fascinated to learn about why they do their particular rituals, because there is always a reason. In *The Power of Myth*, author Joseph Campbell speaks about the purpose of rituals and ceremonies in aboriginal cultures. He points out commonalities in rituals like circumcision and marriage in such diverse cultures as India, The Congo and Malaysia:

Writes Campbell: "Ceremonies are an expression of Maasai culture and self-determination. Every ceremony is considered a new life. And so they are rites of passage, which every Maasai child is eager to go through. According to the Maasai Association, a community-based non-profit organization working to preserve Maasai culture, the ceremonies include Enkipaata (senior boy ceremony), Emuratta (circumcision), Enkiama (marriage), Eunoto (warrior-shaving ceremony), Eokoto e-kule (milk-drinking ceremony), Enkang oo-nkiri (meat-eating ceremony), Orngesherr (junior elder ceremony), and more."

One ritual of the tribe is lion hunting, which is viewed by the Maasai society as bravery and achievement. If you go on a safari, the guides say, "When a lion meets a Maasai in the jungle, the lion is the one who runs!"

Unfortunately, many of the Maasai initiations and rituals have been eroding due to outside influences. The people there have been told to abandon their way of life and to embrace western ways of life. As a result, this culture remains uncertain in the face of modernism, western religion, and environmental challenges. According to Maasai belief: "It takes one day to destroy a house; to build a new house will take months and perhaps years. If we abandon our way of life to construct a new one, it will take thousands of years."

Learning to understand different cultures and their particular rituals is how we begin to practice compassion. There is so much richness in rituals since they are thousands of years old – something we have lost in our civilized society. Speaking from personal experience, I can tell you that without ritual, I would never have made it through those early days when Tariq died. I learned then that when we are compassionate, we are automatically interested in learning more about other cultures. But when we are in judgment, we might call rituals "crude" or "barbaric."

COMPASSIONATE PEOPLE LISTEN

All human beings want to be accepted. We all have the desire to be loved and to love. If you are compassionate, acceptance will automatically be there and other people will mirror that for you. That is because compassion is contagious. If you have a compassionate heart, people will accept you more easily because compassion is your true nature. All you need to do is practice.

An easy way to practice compassion is to make a commitment to yourself before interacting with others that you will be compassionate with everyone you meet.

You can do this very simply by asking those you meet three questions. Compassionate people talk less about themselves and listen more to other people. Since most people like to talk about themselves, these three questions are a good way to get to know someone. If they don't ask you questions back, don't feel badly about it. They may do so later. But often, after you ask these questions, the other person will ask about you and a genuine connection is achieved.

Pick any three from the following six or make up your own:

- What are you reading now?
- What kind of hobbies do you have?
- Where were you born?
- Why do you live here now?
- How many siblings do you have?
- What do you do?

The bottom line here is to avoid self-indulgence and judgments. Keep in mind that everyone is going through his or her own evolution. All you need to do is listen, which will deepen your ability to feel what they feel. This is the way to get to a higher vibratory frequency. You may have started at *Compassion 101,* but you are working your way to *Compassion 10,001.*

COMPASSION HAS NO LIMITS

Each of our encounters with other people helps to deepen our compassion. There are no limits to how far we can go. I often tell people who have lost family members, "There's nothing quite so painful as a broken heart, but a broken heart is an open heart."

I recently gave a talk in Michigan to a group of parents who had lost one or more of their children. At the end of my talk, a man approached me and said, Your quote reminded me of a quote by Rumi: "God will break your heart over and over and over and over and over and over and over and over again – until it stays open."

It is important to keep your heart open all the time because without an open heart, you cannot have compassion. But if you can learn to live with an open heart, a gentle transformation begins to happen, and there is no limit to how open you can become. It is natural to shut down when you are upset and to close your heart to protect yourself from pain. But the truth, as odd as it sounds, is that the only way to make sure your heart is not broken is to keep it open. A closed heart creates a judging human being, but an open heart never judges.

I have learned throughout my life that if you close your heart, God will break it. So if your heart is breaking a lot, you may want to reflect on this. Do you close your heart too often? I have found that meditation is a good way to open my heart, as well as the practice of compassion, which, by its very nature, requires an open heart.

Rabbi Sheila Peltz Weinberg says, "Just as a tennis player must learn to pay attention to their stance and placement of their elbow and wrist, so we who train the heart need to pay attention to our thoughts and our words and our actions..."

Another word for paying attention is "mindfulness." According to Wikipedia, mindfulness is "having a calm awareness of one's body functions, feelings, content of consciousness, and consciousness itself." Mindfulness plays a central role in the Buddha's teachings where it is affirmed that "correct" or "right" mindfulness is a critical factor in the path to liberation and subsequent peace and enlightenment.

It was Albert Schweitzer who said, "Until he extends his circle of compassion to include all living things, man will not find peace."

CHAPTER NINE
PEACE

Sustained goodwill creates friendship; sustained friendship creates trust;

Sustained trust creates empathy; sustained empathy creates compassion;

And sustained compassion creates peace.

~ Azim Khamisa, Peace Formula

HOW DO WE KNOW THAT PEACE IS POSSIBLE?

How do I know that peace is possible? My answer is, "I know because I am at peace." This is a message that I keep coming back to and is often my closing statement during keynote speeches.

I have spent many years sharing my soul's journey with millions of kids and adults around the world. Millions of tears have been shed, millions of letters have been written, and millions of hearts have opened. I stand before school children, prisoners locked behind bars, families who have lost loved ones, social activists working for peace and justice, and individuals from all socioeconomic backgrounds and faiths who feel helpless and broken-hearted. By sharing my journey, I bring hope. And hope is necessary for peace to be possible.

How do I know? There is only one way to know anything – direct experience. I am NOW at peace. I have experienced first-hand how forgiveness works at restoring peace and how forgiveness works for Tony and his family. And so, I know without a doubt that it can work for you and your family, for our country and indeed it can work for the entire world. Bringing this message to as many people on the planet as possible has become my mantra and my mission in life, the same message that I've brought to schools, prisons and churches throughout the latter part of my life.

I am also bringing that message into corporations and organizations which are environments made up of people who want to create unity in management teams and increase passionate performance. The organization, TKF, is based on the core values of Integrity, Compassionate Confrontation and Forgiveness. Our staff is so passionate about our mission that despite the recent need to reduce salaries, production and performance have increased. Our staff and the board continue to go way beyond what is expected. I focus on this aspect in my lectures with organizations – the role and importance of "High Performance Leadership." I know that this work will create a better climate within companies because where there is redemption, compassionate confrontation, and forgiveness, there is also a better bottom line. When we all work together, productivity increases and people contribute at their zenith. When we feel good about our work and our environment and the culture of the organization, it becomes more than a 9-to-5 job. Our work becomes a part of us and we feel connected to and a part of its success.

While forgiveness has not traditionally been practiced in the corporate environment, I am bringing it there, and it is proving a very valuable tool for managers to learn. I believe that to be a high performance leader, forgiveness plays an essential role.

"From conflict, love and unity are possible" is TKF's sixth key message. When we need to forgive, a journey to peace can begin like it did for me. When we learn to transcend and transform our deepest hurts, hurts that many would judge as unforgivable, then we can transmute lower vibratory emotions into the highest vibrations that restore wholeness, unity and peace. Forgiveness, therefore, is essential for personal, national and planetary peace. I am at peace with the tragic loss of my son only because I was able to spiritually understand and transform it.

I can see now that Tariq's mission was to put me on my spiritual path – to create TKF and to teach forgiveness and peace – very different work than what I was doing before the tragedy. I can hardly believe that I can say without reservation that Tariq's death had a silver lining. The choice I made in 1995 was the right one for me when I forgave instead of seeking revenge. It is only because I responded with empathy, compassion and forgiveness in light of my son's murder, and because of the work I am doing as a result, that Tariq's death holds great spiritual meaning for me. I believe now that Tariq's life was complete and mine as yet, is not. That is why I am still alive and I still have work to do. All of us who are living are not complete and we all still have work to do.

PEACE BEGINS FROM WITHIN

The key point to which I always return is that we can all be at peace, but we will not find it if we look outside of ourselves. Peace is a state of being that begins from within. It is a state of submission, of knowing you are on your path, irrespective of the hit you've just received. When Tariq died I thought my life was over, and at one point I became suicidal. In mythology, a phoenix is an immortal bird. When it dies, it supposedly bursts into flames and is reborn from its own ashes. "To rise from the ashes of the phoenix" signifies the ability to make an incredible comeback after going through what has been called the "dark night of the soul." At times, I feel I have had to traverse this dark night, returning from the ashes.

When you embark on a spiritual path, you are entering into a partnership with your Source – God, Spirit, The Universe, The Divine or however you describe your higher power. I believe that a hidden hand orchestrates everything that I do and that makes me feel at peace.

In partnership with your highest power, there is nothing you can't do. When you move through life, you will feel at peace and that you are doing the work that you were meant to do – God's work. Just remember that when things are not working in your life, it's God's way of getting your attention and providing clues about your purpose. In every conflict, try to see yourself moving closer to your spiritual mission.

YOUR SPIRITUAL JOURNEY

All the things that happen to us in relationships or with co-workers or even with complete strangers, lead us to our spiritual purpose. Not everybody knows what their spiritual purpose is, but there are always clues. When people ask me about finding their spiritual purpose, I tell them that we are all here to serve, and along the totem pole of humanity, kids come first. Children rely on us. So although I can't tell anyone their specific spiritual purpose, I know it will fall under the umbrella of serving humanity and the planet. Albert Schweitzer said, "I don't know what your destiny will be, but one thing I know: The only ones among you who will be truly happy, are those who have sought and found how to serve."

When we serve others, it is in the giving that we receive. Through the simple telling of my story, I have inadvertently been instrumental in healing and impacting millions of kids in schools, inmates in prisons, and working adults. With a humble heart, I have been blessed to receive over 100,000 letters, e-mails, and testimonials, most of which express an awakened sense of gratitude and an opening of the heart to empathy, compassion, forgiveness, peace, and love. Knowing that people, especially children, have been transformed by my message is what keeps me motivated, inspired, and energized. I know that if we can all get to a place of peace within ourselves, it will have an amazing impact on the planet.

Martin Luther King, Jr. said, "An individual has not started living until he can rise above the narrow confines of his individualistic concerns to the broader concerns of all humanity."

Those of you doing this work are the trailblazers, creating a path of peace for people to follow, so continue using your voice and stand up for peace as we work together and help each other. In

1952, Mildred Lisette Norman, an American pacifist, vegetarian, and peace activist, became the first woman to walk the entire length of the Appalachian Trail in one season. This same woman, commencing on January 1, 1953 in Pasadena, California, adopted the name "Peace Pilgrim" and walked across the United States for 28 years. Her only possessions were the clothes on her back and the few items she carried in the pockets of her blue tunic which read "Peace Pilgrim" on the front and "25,000 Miles on Foot for Peace" on the back. She had no organizational backing, no money, and never asked for food or shelter. At the start of her pilgrimage, she took a vow "to remain a wanderer until mankind has learned the way of peace, walking until given shelter and fasting until given food." Her philosophy was, "One little person, giving all of her time to peace makes news. Many people, giving some of their time, can make history."

Helen Keller said, "I am only one; still I am one. I cannot do everything, but still I can do something. I will not refuse to do something I can do."

Along with many trailblazers who came before us, we must also acknowledge the remarkable spirits that continue to help us right now. I know that Tariq is very involved with this work, obviously not on a physical plane, but rather on the spiritual plane. I always feel the spirits of people helping me at TKF and my other organization CANEI. These spirits are trying to make this a better world and to make us better people.

I have always found Gandhi's spirit to be a guiding light. He said, "You must not lose faith in humanity. Humanity is an ocean; if a few drops of the ocean are dirty, the ocean does not become dirty." If we take the time to contemplate the words of the greatest influencers for peace, we will understand their convictions and their passion will become our own."

SAMADHI AND ONENESS

Much like forgiveness, peace is about peeling back the layers of the onion and working to uncover newer and more refined qualities of peace and bliss. As you do more of this work, you will find that your meditations become more profound and you will experience an even deeper sense of peace. There is no limit to where you can go. You will able to get into the "gap" more and enter a profound state called "Samadhi" – where there is no thought or mantra. It is a very peaceful, loving, blissful place to be.

Wikipedia defines Samadhi as: "a Buddhist and Hindu term that denotes higher levels of concentrated meditation. In Hinduism, it is the eighth and final limb of the Yoga Sutra of Patanjali. It has been described as a non-dualistic state of consciousness in which the consciousness of the experiencing subject becomes one with the experienced object and in which the mind becomes still though the person remains conscious."

I believe that Samadhi, a place of peace, is somewhere we can all get to. It arises from the understanding that we are on our spiritual mission, that we are on purpose, that God or the Universe or whatever or whomever one believes in, is with us. Samadhi is the notion that we are part of a universal consciousness and within that universal consciousness, we are doing what we are here to do. As a result, we are able to experience deeper meditations and get to a deeper state of peace.

Arjuna Ardagh is an author, speaker and founder of the Living Essence Foundation in Nevada City, California, a non-profit church dedicated to "the awakening of consciousness within the context of ordinary life." He writes in his book, *Awakening Into Oneness,* "Because of the phenomenon of a 'tipping point,' only a relatively small percentage of the world's population needs to shift from separation to Oneness for the whole planet to shift."

The important thing for those of us on this path is to remember that we are all connected – we are all one. The source that we all come from is the same. The soul is ancient; it existed long before the world was created so all the divisions we see are man-made. When you are in the gap, you transcend all that stuff. You go back to the source where there is no difference between you and me. What you have in you is the same thing I have in me and this applies to everyone. Religion, race, color, age, gender and nationality issues do not exist. There is no rich or poor, black or white, male or female. In transcending this, we really feel we are one.

I had that feeling with Tony. Even though he took the life of my son, my soul connected with his and I was able to recognize that we were one. In my book, *"The Secrets of the Bulletproof Spirit,"* there is a chapter entitled, "When You See With Real Eyes You Realize." I understood that Tony and I came from the same spark that was here before the universe – a spark of eternal, ever-expanding love.

Elizabeth Kubler Ross, psychiatrist and author of the groundbreaking book *On Death and Dying* said, "If we could see that everything, even tragedy, is a gift in disguise, we would then find the best way to nourish the soul."

The soul never dies. Tariq is at home. He's not dead because there is really no such thing as death. We are all eventually going to be where Tariq is, and I feel him with me. So when you die, the spirit, life force, or "prana" – there are many words for it – leaves the body. But while we are alive, we can connect with it. So why don't we?

I believe it's because we spend 99.9 percent of the time in our heads instead of our hearts. And I'm no different – except when I meditate. That is when I feel like I'm dancing with spirit, which is what meditation is all about. When we are in the gap – the Samadhi state – we become one with source – an amazing state of bliss.

The more we practice being with the source, the more we feel a deep sense of connectedness. The Dalai Lama is an inspiring example of someone living from spirit all the time. He stays in a state of great humility, purity and peace, and we can get a sense of it when we practice. When we are a living example of all of the virtues that this book is focusing on, we are at peace and it radiates out to every living being. While I am basically at peace with Tariq's death, I fall off the wagon and as they say, my feathers get ruffled. But I turn to my spiritual practice and increase my meditation as soon as I can so I can get back on the wagon – back to peace. If everyone knew how beneficial a daily practice can be, they would all be doing it!

DAILY PRACTICE

This incredible quote is from an unknown source: "When your life is filled with the desire to see holiness in everyday life, something magical happens, ordinary life becomes extraordinary, and the very process of life begins to nourish your soul!"

Though I start each day with a prayer and a reading, most of my spiritual practice is meditation, probably about 95 percent. There are still many different methods to perform a daily spiritual practice such as: prayer, saying affirmations, reading inspirational literature, listening to music, doing yoga, being out in nature, journaling – anything that takes you from outside yourself and places you back inside your heart. Sunsets, for instance, can be very arresting and cause you to feel as if you are out of your body and mind.

Looking at the stars and the Milky Way puts me in touch with my source because these sights are so magnificent. The mountains, the Taj Mahal, and a full moon have that kind of majestic impact on me.

I highly recommend at least an hour of meditation or some other spiritual way of reconnecting with source. I find when I don't get my meditation in, it's as if I'm walking on sea legs, wobbly and off balance. That's when I know I need to slow down. With all my travel and speaking engagements, life can start to feel overwhelming and there are days where I don't get my two hours in. I don't like those days. When I do get my two hours in, I feel centered, calm and at peace. Things flow and all is well.

Today's world is so busy – busy – busy. But oftentimes, we stay busy because we're hiding from the real stuff in our lives. Busy-ness can be a mask for what's really going on. But when we meditate, contemplate, and look introspectively at our issues, we cannot hide. This is why alone time is so important. For people who feel they cannot meditate, they can still spend time in reflection and contemplation. A silent retreat can be powerful and transformative while something as simple as journaling can be an amazing tool to reconnect with spirit or source. It doesn't matter how long you engage in your spiritual practice. Two hours a day works well for me, but you can do twenty minutes or three hours, whatever works for you. The point is that doing this twice a day will bring you the best results. In the morning, we have the opportunity to go into the gap and manifest the day. In the evening, we have the opportunity to process what took place during the day.

I suggest listening to a free guided meditation on discovering one's spiritual purpose. It can be found on my homepage of my website: AzimKhamisa.com.

SIMPLIFY

Henry David Thoreau said, "As you simplify your life, the laws of the universe will be simpler; solitude will not be solitude, poverty will not be poverty, nor weakness weakness."

We have all heard that less is more. But most of us don't believe it. We tend to have overly-complicated lives because it is human nature to try to achieve. And so, we take on more and more. I have certainly been guilty of this. In the book, *The Way of The Peaceful Warrior*, author Dan Millman writes, "The secret of happiness is not found in seeking more, but in developing the capacity to enjoy less."

While I know that my efforts in this life are important, I also know that I must strive for balance and simplicity – and to not always be working. Having a social life is essential to anyone's peace and happiness. A colleague and a good friend of mine teaches "integration" instead of focusing on balance. Integration of all that fulfills us while keeping our lives simple is something we can all achieve with mindfulness and dedication.

To begin, ask yourself, "What can I do to simplify my life?" It may become apparent, as it has for me, that you have to take some things off your plate. I learned the hard way that I am much better off focusing on doing one thing really well than on doing a million little things not so well. As Americans, our tendency is to do more, to overachieve, to keep busy, and to measure success by accomplishments and our external acquisitions. Most of us do not have simple lives. Robert Frost made an interesting point when he said, "By working hard eight hours a day, you may eventually get to be boss and work hard twelve hours a day."

The older I get, the more the idea of simplifying appeals to me. I constantly search for what I can eliminate. If you want to do this, too, ask yourself, "What do I really love? What brings me joy, happiness, and peace? Can I do without the rest? Can I make enough money doing what I really love?" If you focus on doing that which you really love, you may be able to do just that.

In the spiritual classic, *I AM THAT*, Indian spiritual teacher and philosopher of Advaita (Non-dualism), Sri Nisagardatta Maharaj, says, "Once you realize that the road is the goal and that you are always on the road, not to reach a goal, but to enjoy its beauty and its wisdom, life ceases to be a task and becomes natural and simple, in itself an ecstasy."

Nisargadatta offers four "austerities" that when followed, can bring clarity, focus, simplicity, joy, bliss, and peace:

1. Don't repeat mistakes.
2. Avoid the unnecessary.
3. Live an orderly life.

4. Don't anticipate pleasure or pain.

These four austerities may look and sound easy at first glance. But I challenge you to be mindful of these four seemingly simple invitations. You may want to print them out, tape them to your computer, or carry them in your wallet as a reminder. Focus, focus, focus on these four austerities, and you will be amazed at what comes into your awareness.

One way to simplify your life is take a break or, as it is called, go on sabbatical. A good definition for sabbatical is: "resembling the Sabbath; enjoying or bringing an intermission of labor." The idea of taking a hiatus or a sabbatical is one way to refocus and reflect on what is truly important. Many of us have been so busy for so long that we are fast approaching "burn-out." Our culture does not do a very good job at making peace a priority or a focus for our lives. Thus, many of us are running around like chickens with our heads cut off, feeling stressed, ill and totally out of touch with what matters most.

Taking a break helps us to refocus our energy as it all begins to flow in one direction. Then we can accomplish things quicker, easier, and with more satisfaction. Then we can be peaceful.

On the other hand, when energy is divided into many directions, this fragmentation results in anxiety and stress. I have a wonderful quote posted on my wall by Margret Thatcher from her tribute to Ronald Reagan on his 80th birthday:

"It takes struggles in life to make strength. It takes fight for principles to make fortitude. It takes crises to give courage. And it takes singleness of purpose to reach an objective."

FOCUSING ON PEACE

Louise Diamond, author of *The Peace Book*, writes: "The journey for peace – inner peace and peace on earth – is ultimately a spiritual journey. Our souls long for peace. Our spirit hungers to its source, where peace and love reside unconditionally. When we remember our natural self, we swim in this essence."

The burning question is: How do we focus on peace when presented with angry, rude, disrespectful, abrasive, annoying, self-centered, sandpaper-to-the soul people?

The answer is: Practice, practice, practice.

What initially might seem counter-intuitive, such as sending love and forgiveness to someone with whom we are in conflict, eventually becomes second nature. This is why having a spiritual foundation and a daily practice is so vital. It is easy to love people who love us. But Jesus said, "You have heard that it was said, Love your neighbor and hate your enemy. But I tell you: Love your enemies and pray for those who persecute you. If you love those who love you, what reward will you get? Are not even the tax collectors doing that?"

Our greatest reward comes in loving those who are difficult to love. When we focus on practicing the ideals in this book, we will learn not only to temper emotional reactions such as anger, judgment, resentment, and blame, we will learn to transcend them. Through practice, we will be able to easily and quickly detach from that which may initially appear personal and return to our true nature, which is compassionate, peaceful, and loving. When conflicts arise – as they will – we will stay centered in peace, the way that the Dalai Lama and other enlightened beings live.

You can begin by noticing when you are not at peace with the situations and relationships in your life. You can decide to do things that will help bring more peace to yourself and to anyone you have had an issue or conflict with. When a conflict arises, rather than stew over it and justify why another is wrong or has harmed you, you can look within and ask yourself, "Why have I attracted this into my life? How can I learn and grow from this experience?"

If you cultivate this awareness – that what you attract in your life is for your spiritual growth – then it becomes easier to take a step back, look within and ask yourself, "Why did I attract this? What is this conflict, struggle or experience trying to teach me on a deeper, spiritual level?"

PEACE IS ALWAYS POSSIBLE

No matter what transpires, peace is always possible because peace is a choice. To return to peace, you must be dedicated to peace. What is the alternative? There is nothing profound about the path of peace. Peace is always there. It is simply a matter of reconnecting with your deepest self – the very essence of who you are.

There are many ways to do this as I have mentioned earlier – taking a walk in nature, journaling, praying, or meditating on peace. You always have a choice to stop being angry, take a time-out, and breathe deeply in order to calm yourself. Your breath is a powerful force in helping you find peace. With each deep breath, simply say the word "peace" or "love" as you inhale and exhale. Focus your attention on your heart as you breathe in and out "peace" and "love." Not only is this a good practice for you; it is also a great thing for children to experience as they drift off to sleep.

Once you reconnect with your peaceful, loving nature, you can send love and forgiveness to anyone whom you may have hurt or who has hurt you or your loved ones. Silently you can thank the most challenging of people for helping you on your journey to compassion, empathy, forgiveness, peace and love.

You can acknowledge the role of those who have caused you pain as your life's greatest teachers. You can see every experience with new eyes and appreciate the challenges that have been brought forth for your spiritual growth. You can become a witness to any emotional reaction you may have had. You can release any emotions and forgive yourself and others for everything. You can invite the divine to help you at any time. You can ask for clarity and wisdom. You can surrender to the highest good for all. You can know that everything is part of a divine plan for the highest good. You can feel waves of peace wash over you. You can smile and say "thank you" for all that is. Thank you for showing me the way back to my soul – to the place where peace and love reside.

To be at peace is to love all that is. Love is to be at peace with all that is. Hafiz said, "We are people who need to love, because Love is the soul's life. Love is simply creation's greatest joy."

May we all continue on our own individual journeys in our own individual ways to practice forgiveness with ourselves and others; to extend goodwill to everyone; to build trust and deepen friendships and to experience empathy. May we continue to think, speak, and act with compassion; to find fulfillment through living out our spiritual purpose; to live in love and gratitude for everything and everyone; to know peace, to live peace; and to be at peace. This is my hope, my desire, my meditation, and my eternal prayer.

EPILOGUE

A CONTEMPLATION ON PEACE

Teach this triple truth to all: A generous heart, kind speech, and a life of service and compassion are the things which renew humanity.

- The Buddha

And so the journey is complete ... for now.

We have traveled from fulfillment to peace in this book, and all the way from murder to peace in the full trilogy of the journey. With each step, we have learned much, as each step carries its own purpose, lessons and empowerment – all holding the seed of peace. All along, peace has been a destination, and it has been met through goodwill, friendship, trust, empathy, forgiveness and compassion.

A wonderful poem by Black Elk, Oglala Sioux and Spiritual Leader, outlines the path of peace:

THE TRUE PEACE

The first peace, which is the most important,

Is that which comes within the souls of people

When they realize their relationship,

Their oneness, with the universe and all its powers,

And when they realize that at the center

Of the universe dwells Wakan-Taka (the Great Spirit),

And that this center is really everywhere, it is within each of us.

This is the real peace, and the others are but reflections of this.

The second peace is that which is made between two individuals,

And the third is that which is made between two nations.

But above all you should understand that there can never

Be peace between nations until there is known that true peace,

Which, as I have often said, is within the souls of men.

This higher picture helps us truly see the expansive nature of peace – it is not simply for our own calm mind. It expands from there to influence and impact our family, friends, community and society, as well as everyone we meet. It can all start with us. And often it all starts with a true and deep desire, a prayer. One such prayer, or affirmation, comes from Unity Magazine:

UNITY'S DAILY WORD - WORLD PEACE

With hearts united in love, we bless our world and envision peace for all people. There is a new world continually unfolding, and each day is one of renewed faith. We act on divine guidance to further world peace. One by one, right where we are, we take individual peace-centered actions that create a convergence of harmony. We are patient in traffic or in customer waiting lines. We are understanding of one another's feelings. We listen before offering our own input and suggestions. We contribute our time or material gifts to those in need of assistance. Each thought, word, and action is a demonstration of peace and harmony. Throughout the world, with like-minded hearts and souls, we link our prayers and love to bless all people of the world.

Within this book of peace, I endeavored to share a path with you. It was a path rich with wisdom from others on their own paths of enlightenment. With each chapter, the intention was to point you towards those emotions that are of a high vibratory rate. From the likes of the Dalai Lama, I learned that individuals not operating at this high vibratory state are quick to judgment, anger, avarice, backbiting, gossip, resentment – often encountering very low vibratory emotions. I've learned that we must train ourselves to live in high vibratory levels, and these include forgiveness, love, and peacemaking, because happiness lives in the high vibratory emotions.

I invite you all to put into practice the steps held within each chapter, for each chapter's topics are of that high vibration. If you do, you will remain in that higher state longer and thus simply find the path to happiness and peace.

Even though it's a simple path before us, I do recognize that we all have a bad hair day every once in a while. I have my own bad days. And sometimes I fall off the wagon. At those times when I recognize myself falling into a lower thought-pattern or lower minded way of being, I acknowledge that I've fallen and then take action to readjust my trajectory, often times adding an additional 30 minutes of meditation to my daily spiritual practice.

It's so vital to consistently catch yourself when you dip, and commit to spending more and more time in the higher vibratory state so you will have longer periods of happiness and peace. Perhaps we aren't there yet, like the Dalai Lama who lives there 24/7, but we can make a conscious effort to distinguish on a daily and hourly basis our present state, and make our choices of where we want and need to be. All it takes is the choice and the will, and then the surrender to a higher path awaiting us.

Here is a beautiful poem by Rabindranath Tagore, who asks for strength to surrender to the divine:

GIVE ME STRENGTH

This is my prayer to thee, my lord – strike, strike at the root of penury in my heart.

Give me the strength lightly to bear my joys and sorrows.

Give me the strength to make my love fruitful in service.

Give me the strength never to disown the poor or bend my knees before insolent might.

Give me the strength to raise my mind high above daily trifles.

And give me the strength to surrender my strength to thy will with love.

We all carry, I believe, such a will for the good and for the divine, and it's a will to expand beyond our lower selves and realize the higher-self dwelling within. If we all become better people, then we will create a better planet and enjoy a world at peace. I truly believe that peace within each and every one of us on an individual level is possible, and the intention of this book was to provide a recipe to get there. When we find peace within ourselves, we will radiate this peace within our families and our circles of influence because it is contagious. I am reminded of this short, sweet poem by Hafiz called *The Happy Virus*: "I caught the happy virus last night when I was out singing beneath the stars. It is remarkably contagious – So kiss me."

Being at peace is good for our health. When we are at peace, we sleep better, and we can move into deeper levels of meditation as we tap into our consciousness. That's really what this work is all about. St. Francis of Assisi's famous prayer eloquently illustrates the concept of surrendering to the service of humanity for the highest and greatest good for all:

PRAYER OF ST. FRANCIS

Lord, make me an instrument of your peace;

Where there is hatred, let me sow love;

Where there is injury, pardon;

Where there is doubt, faith;

Where there is despair, hope;

Where there is darkness, light;

And where there is sadness, joy.

O Divine Master,

Grant that I may not so much seek to be consoled as to console;

To be understood, as to understand;

To be loved, as to love;

For it is in giving that we receive,

It is in pardoning that we are pardoned,

And it is in dying that we are born to Eternal Life.

And so it is time to say our farewell. It's been a great journey, from fulfillment to peace. Thank you for taking it with me. It is in the sharing that we realize the path we are truly on. I share this path of peace, and conclude with a word of thanks, a word of gratitude, and a word known to all who share in the one unity: Namaste.

NAMASTE

I honor the place in you

In which the entire universe dwells

I honor the place in you

Which is of love,

Of truth, of light,

And of peace

When you are in

That place in you,

And I am in that

Place in me,

We are one

RESOURCES

OTHER WORKS BY AZIM KHAMISA

BOOKS
- *Azim's Bardo - From Murder to Forgiveness* (Published by Balboa Press – a subsidiary of Hay House)
- *From Forgiveness to Fulfillment*
- *The Secrets of the Bullet-proof Spirit* (Random House Publishing, Spring 2009)

CDs
Tapestry – The Audio Series
Forgiveness – The Crown Jewel of Personal Freedom
    (3-Disk Series and Workbook)

DVDs
Tapestry – The Video Series
From Murder to Forgiveness (Chariot Productions)
Garden of Life

See complete list at www.AzimKhamisa.com.

TKF

The Tariq Khamisa Foundation (TKF)
4025 Camino Del Rio South, Suite 100, San Diego, CA 92108
(858) 565-0800
www.tkf.org
- *In Class Curriculum*
- *After School Groups / Mentoring*
- *Safe School Model*
- *Ending the Cycle of Violence video series*
- *Violence Impact Assembly*
- *Seeds of Hope Society*

AZIM KHAMISA

Azim N. Khamisa
www.AzimKhamisa.com
(858) 452-6849
- *Speaking*
- *Workshops*
- *Products of Forgiveness and Peace*

CHILD SAFETY NETWORK

President: Azim Khamisa
5205 Kearny Villa Way, #103
San Diego, CA 92123
(800) 906-6901 x16

CANEI, NYAP, AND YAPI

CANEI (Constant and Never Ending Improvement)
See www.AzimKhamisa.com

NYAP (National Youth Advocate Program)
Mubarak Awad and William Espinosa
1801 Watermark Drive, Suite 200, Columbus, OH 43215

(614) 487.8758 | (877) NYAP-CAN (692-7226)
www.nyap.org

YAPI (Youth Advocate Program International, Inc.)
Mubarak Awad
4000 Albemarle St. NW, Suite 401, Washington, DC 20016
www.yapi.org
(202) 244-6410

RESTORATIVE JUSTICE

Center for Restorative Justice and Peacemaking at the School of
Social Work, University of Minnesota
1404 Gortner Ave, 105 Peters Hall
St. Paul, MN 55108-6160
(612) 624-4923
rjp.umn.edu/index.html

VORP (Victim-Offender Reconciliation Program)
Information and Resource Center
PO Box 306
Asheville, NC 28802
(828) 301-6211
www.vorp.com

Loyola Marymount University
Center for Restorative Justice
Scott Wood
919 Albany Street
Los Angeles, CA 90015
(213) 736-8301

PEACE, FORGIVENESS and VIOLENCE PREVENTION

The Peace Alliance (Establishing a US Department of Peace)
www.ThePeaceAlliance.org

Marianne Williamson's website:
www.marianne.com

Dr. Michael Beckwith
Agape International Spiritual Center
5700 Buckingham Parkway
Culver City, CA 90230
(310) 348-1250
www.agapelive.com

Children's Defense Fund / Ward Leber
25 E Street NW
Washington DC 20001
(800) 233-1200
www.childrensdefense.org

M.K. Gandhi Institute for Nonviolence
929 S. Plymouth Ave.
Rochester, New York 14608
Phone (585) 463-3266
Fax (585) 276-0203
www.GandhiInstitute.org

Chariot Videos: Victress Hitchcock
3051 Madeline St., Oakland, CA 94602
Phone (510) 479-3017
Fax (719) 362-4213
Email info@chariotvideos.com
www.ChariotVideos.com

PERSONAL DEVELOPMENT

Klemmer & Associates, Inc., Leadership and Character
Development
1340 Commerce St, Suite G
Petaluma, CA 94954
(800) 577-5447
www.klemmer.com

Senn-Delaney Leadership
3780 Kilroy Airport Way, Suite 800
Long Beach, CA 90806
(562) 426-5400
www.senndelaney.com

Belinda Farrell
Ho'oponopono / HUNA / Author of *Find Your Friggin' Joy*
PO Box 3923, Santa Cruz, CA 95063
(866) 583-8370
www.hunahealing.com

25073381R00083

Made in the USA
San Bernardino, CA
16 October 2015